THE INTERMEDIATE
GUIDE TO RAISING CHICKENS

THE INTERMEDIATE GUIDE TO

RAISING CHICKENS

HOW TO EXPAND AND MAINTAIN A HAPPY BACKYARD FLOCK

AMBER BRADSHAW

ROCKRIDGE
PRESS

For general information on our other products and services or to obtain technical support, please contact our Customer Care Department within the United States at (866) 744-2665, or outside the United States at (510) 253-0500.

Rockridge Press publishes its books in a variety of electronic and print formats. Some content that appears in print may not be available in electronic books, and vice versa.

Interior and Cover Designer: Jill Lee
Art Producer: Sue Bishofberger
Associate Editor: Maxine Marshall
Production Editor: Matt Burnett
Production Manager: Riley Hoffman

Illustrations © 2021 Annalisa Durante and Marina Durante, cover and pp. vii, x-xii, 12, 21, 26, 28, 30, 39, 41, 44, 53, 54-56, 59, 67, 73, 76, 77, 84, 106, 115, 117, 121, 123, 128; © Benlin Alexander, pp. iii, 22, 42, 62, 75, 81, 82, 104, and 110.

ISBN: Print 978-1-648-76966-5 | eBook 978-1-648-76967-2
R0

TO MY HUSBAND, TIMMY, AND OUR THREE
CHILDREN, GAVIN, MORGAN, AND LINDEN

CONTENTS

INTRODUCTION

I'm Amber Bradshaw, and I live in the mountains of East Tennessee, where my family and I stay off-grid on our developing 47-acre farm. However, I didn't always live this way. We started our little homestead journey in a popular tourist area at the beach, where the climate was humid and tropical. Our tiny flock began with just a couple of backyard chickens on no more than one-tenth of an acre of land.

I was first introduced to raising chickens as a young child living with my grandparents in Southern California. My grandmother was the original chicken whisperer, and she never met an animal or insect that she didn't consider a friend.

Even with my grandparents' example, it wasn't until later in my adult years that I realized how much I valued the idea of raising my family's food and becoming self-sufficient. Sadly, by that time, my grandparents were no longer around to share their wisdom. I was left on my own to learn through trials, failures, and mistakes. Those hard experiences were my teacher—and, boy, have I learned a lot of lessons.

One of those early lessons related to the projected egg counts you find when you're looking up breed statistics. You know, when you're on the hatchery website looking at breeds and the descriptions says, "Great layer; 250 to 300 eggs per year." Those egg statistics? Well, I did my calculations and ordered just enough pullets (young females) to provide my family with fresh eggs daily and have enough left over to sell to friends. Are you laughing at me yet? Or maybe you're nodding because you're right there with me? Long story short, we ended up going to the store numerous times to buy eggs during that first year because the girls decided not to lay. It was too hot, it was too cold, they were in molt, the neighbors' noise stressed them out, the sun wasn't bright enough, I forgot to give them treats . . . whatever the reason, they went on strike—a LOT.

After more than a decade of similar lessons, I can confidently say that there is always something to learn when it comes to animals. I often look back at my chicken-keeping experience and laugh at my beginner days. I was so naive and Google smart, with no practical life experience and no one close to me to ask for guidance. I was grabbing life by the feathers and felt determined to single-handedly provide all my family's food on just one-tenth of an acre.

This book is all about moving beyond that first year, because unless it becomes dinner for you or some unknown predator, a chicken's average life span is close to that of a dog. Now that you've made a few mistakes of your own and understand that you're in it for the long haul, it's time to take raising chickens to the next level.

In these pages, I'm going to do for you what I wish someone had done for me back in the day. I'm going to take you past that first year of chicken-raising— and maybe some crushed expectations—and bring you into a successful second year and beyond. I hope to help you not only thrive with your flock, but maybe even turn it into a sustainable business. Believe it or not, you can sell your eggs and eat 'em, too!

CHAPTER 1
KEEPING YOUR CHICKENS HAPPY

Any livestock or pet owner cares about the well-being of their animals. We are their caregivers, and it's up to us to make sure they live happy and healthy lives. They can only do this through our good animal husbandry, diligence, and observation. To support you on this mission, this chapter discusses the ins and outs of keeping your flock happy and understanding how they tick.

THE CHICKEN-KEEPING LIFE

Regardless of your motivation to join the fresh-eggs club, one thing is clear: Chickens are both rewarding and time-consuming. You may be one of the many who bought into the idea of Pinterest-perfect chicken coops with pretty curtains, clean perches, cute little chicken swings, and even a shiny mirror, only for you to find, months down the road, that everything is covered in chicken poop. Yeah, the Pinterest pictures forget to include the chicken poop.

I was one of those people. I made a beautiful backyard chicken coop with curtains and little pictures in each nesting box and planted an amazing garden just for my chickens. Cue the reality check. After a decade or more of raising chickens of several different breeds, both in an urban environment while negotiating with an HOA and in the country with acres and acres of wildlife, Pinterest-perfect can kiss my fluffy feathered rear. If you've raised chickens for a year or more, you've gone beyond starry-eyed chickens and cocktails; you know things can and will happen. There's a lot more to raising chickens than collecting fresh eggs every day.

Over the years with my flocks, we've had to deal with hurricanes, freezing temperatures, worms, mites, egg eaters, cockfights, predators, bumblefoot, county laws, and so much more. I've had to become an emergency vet, a foster parent, a mortician, a chicken advocate, and a referee. Despite all of this, I wouldn't change a thing. The most beautiful noise I hear in the morning is our roosters crowing, and I love the hens' egg songs during the day. Knowing that we have chickens roaming our land means I have food security for my family, and nothing is better than that.

UNDERSTANDING YOUR CHICKENS

One of the keys to good animal husbandry is observation. Good observation makes it possible to raise a successful flock that enriches not only your chickens' lives but yours as well. Fortunately, observing chickens is no dull task. Chickens are full of flavor, both literally and metaphorically. They are bursting with personality and unique behavioral traits, so much so that people actually pay to watch livestreams of chickens freely roaming the pasture. I kid you not.

By now, you've observed your flock working out its pecking order and have probably learned to distinguish their different calls. But what else can their behaviors teach you? Spending time with your flock doesn't just provide you with endless entertainment; through observation, you can also begin to understand what they are trying to tell you. Many chicken issues—like a lethargic chicken, a chicken who's being pecked on, or an egg-bound hen—can be diagnosed or assessed through simple observation. We will delve into the health-related topics in more detail in chapter 5. For now, let's take a look at your chickens' behavioral traits and what they can teach you about helping your flock operate at its optimum level.

THE HIERARCHY OF CHICKENS' NEEDS

In the early 1940s, a psychologist named Abraham Maslow developed a hierarchical pyramid of human needs. His idea was that when all the needs in the pyramid were met, the human was at their optimum level, performing at their very best. The lower levels of the hierarchy, the basic needs, have to be met before the next level can be achieved. Maslow identified human needs as physical needs first, then safety, then belongingness/love, and then esteem and self-actualization at the top of the pyramid. Self-actualization is when someone is able reach their full potential, something that is only possible once their other, more basic, needs have been met.

This philosophy was adapted by Philip A. Stayer, DVM, MS, ACPV, a veterinarian for a commercial poultry producer, to be applied to chickens. He observed that chickens were much like humans in that they had a hierarchy of needs. When every level of their needs pyramid was met, they were happy, healthy chickens—our ultimate goal. He concluded that a chicken's hierarchy of needs is made up of freedom from predation, thermal comfort, food and water, and, at the top of the pyramid, an opportunity to frolic. Although I'll discuss providing for these needs later on, let's first explore the behaviors associated with each. Remember, the first step in caring for your flock is observing their behaviors and interpreting what those behaviors are telling you.

Chickens' needs pyramid

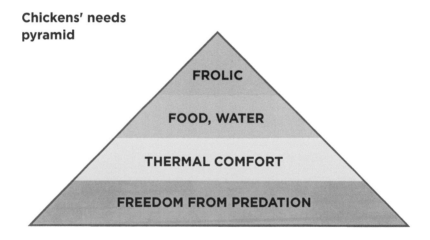

FREEDOM FROM PREDATION

Chickens are pretty much at the bottom of the food chain. Heck, even chickens like eating chicken meat and eggs, if given the chance. Chickens know this and do their best to protect themselves from predators. If your chickens are falling prey to a predator, you probably won't witness the actual attack. Instead, keep an eye out for some behaviors they display when they feel threatened.

Hiding. If you go out in your coop and notice your chickens are missing but there are no feathers on the ground (no more so than normal), chances are your flock is playing chicken and hiding. I have a rooster who we lovingly call Scaredy Rooster. He is at the bottom of the pecking order. Once, a fox attacked our flock and I thought Scaredy Rooster was a goner. We couldn't find him for a whole day. Lo and behold, he was at the back of our cabin with his head tucked behind a water barrel. You could literally see his entire body except for his head. I guess he assumed if he couldn't see the fox, the fox couldn't see him. If you witness this kind of behavior, consider providing your flock with more cover or obstacles to hide in or behind.

Chatting up a storm. As you know, chickens are noisy. I've never met a quiet chicken (at least, not one who was alive). However, there are times when chickens make more racket than normal and are very loud and boisterous. When you hear this, it's time to check the coop, because chances are you have a predator lurking.

Squatting. Chickens will squat to show submission when they come of age to mate. They will also do this when there are signs of predators, especially aerial ones. For example, raptors such as hawks are attracted to movement, so when a chicken spots a hawk, they will squat low to the ground and freeze. If you notice your chickens squatting or see hawks or other flying predators, lock your chickens in their run or coop until the threat is gone.

THERMAL COMFORT

The next level on the chicken needs pyramid is thermal comfort. Temperature extremes can have a great effect on your chickens' health and happiness. Even baby chickens who don't have the right temperature in their brooder will stop eating or drinking. Watch for these behaviors to make sure your flock is comfortable.

Panting. When chickens are hot, much like dogs, they will walk around with their mouths open and pant. There are other health-related issues that would cause a chicken to pant (see chapter 5), but it is good to start by ruling out heat as the problem.

Ruffled feathers. When chickens are hot, they will ruffle their feathers and extend their wings to try to cool down. No need to give them a cold shower, but do make sure they have plenty of water to drink and ample shade. They will also ruffle their feathers when they are cold, which is normal. However, if your chickens constantly have their feathers fluffed out, check their body temperature to make sure they aren't too cold.

Huddling. Chickens will often huddle when they're cold. You can see this when they are fresh out of the egg. In a brooder, you'll notice the baby chicks all huddled together under the heat lamp. Older chickens might be more prone to huddling to keep warm as well. In ideal thermal conditions, your chickens will be all scattered about.

FOOD AND WATER

Once chickens are safe and warm, they must be watered and fed. Chickens need access to fresh food and water 24/7. The only time you should ever withhold either is when you're raising specific meat chickens who would otherwise overeat to the detriment of their health. The following behaviors are associated with food and water and either help you know that your chickens are happily satiated or give you a clue that your flock might be lacking in nutrition.

Attack of the chickens. Chickens are easily trainable and have a great memory when it comes to food sources. If you hand-feed your chickens every day, they will associate you with food or treats. When they see you, they will come running. They aren't attacking, they're hangry. They may even peck at you until you surrender and give them something more to eat.

Egg eating. Egg eating is one of those bad behaviors that chickens develop rather than do instinctively. Chickens eat eggs for several reasons. First, they taste good. The other is that their diet is lacking in nutrition. If you notice that your chickens are enjoying the eggs before you can, make sure they have enough food and water as well as supplements and calcium.

All for me. The play yard bullies (those at the top of the pecking order) have a tendency to hog the food and water. They will push and peck those below them in the hierarchy. If you observe this behavior, add extra feeders and waterers to ensure there is plenty for everyone.

FROLIC

The top tier of the chicken needs pyramid is frolic. Chickens are very social creatures. They need other feathered friends to cohabitate with, and they are happiest when they can range free and peck in the yard or pasture. A chicken's nature is to scratch, peck, and forage. When the ability to frolic is combined with the first three needs, chickens can achieve their full potential. Support that full potential by keeping a careful eye out for these behaviors.

Purring. Have you heard your chickens purr? Similar to cats, chickens make a purring sound when they're happy. Hearing a purr from a hen means your girl is feeling good and her needs are being met.

Whimpering. Chickens get sad, lonely, depressed, and even angry. When a chicken is experiencing one of these emotions, you may hear them whimper.

Feather picking. We used to have a parrot who we inherited when his owner passed away. For months, he would pull his feathers out in grief. Chickens do the same thing when they're bored, lonely, or sad.

CHICKEN ENRICHMENT

Although chickens are far from being a hands-off kind of livestock—as I'm sure you know by now—they are easier to raise and maintain than other livestock. Once you've provided the basics such as shelter, protection, food, and water, it doesn't take lot of extra effort to help your chickens reach their full potential. Let's explore additions or changes you can make to enrich your flock's lives.

MIX UP THE ROUTINE

If your chickens don't have enough room to roam or if their coop is too crowded, you might notice them displaying signs of boredom or depression, including pecking, feather loss, or appetite loss. Bust that boredom with one (or more) of these fun, easy enrichments, which will help your flock live their best chicken lives.

Extend their living quarters. If your chickens are confined to a coop and a run, consider building a chicken tractor (a mobile chicken coop and run) that you can move around daily to give them new land to forage and new scenery to gaze on.

Add mirrors. Chickens love to socialize, even if it's with their own reflection. Livestock suppliers carry shatterproof chicken mirrors that you can hang in the coop.

Plant a chicken garden. Let's face it: If you have a garden and you have chickens, they are going to find it and eat it. Sometimes *all* of it. So, you might as well plant a garden for them. As an added bonus, chickens foraging on fresh fruits and vegetables provide amazing eggs. If you don't have the room to fix up your flock with their own garden, give them access to your garden at the end of the season, and they will do a wonderful job at cleaning it up, tilling the soil, and adding fertilizer.

Install swings or extra perches. The higher the better. When we lived near the beach, we had fun with our perches by collecting driftwood, which we then hung at different levels throughout our chicken run. Chickens also love to swing; hang a 2-inch-diameter branch or dowling with some rope tied through both ends.

Make fun with food. For chickens, part of the enjoyment of eating is the hunt. They love to scavenge logs for bugs and scratch foliage for worms or other creepy crawlies. Imitate this favorite pastime by giving them a rotten log from the woods, hiding worms in their run, or buying them some crickets. Another fun thing to do with food is hanging melons, cabbage, pumpkins, squash, or treats from a string in their run. During the summer, freeze worms or snacks in a block of ice and let them peck at it for their special treat.

Give them dust baths. Chickens bathe by digging in the dirt and then rolling around in it. One of the easiest ways I've found to make them a dust bath (so they don't dig a bunch of holes in my yard) is to provide them with a couple of old tires filled with loose dirt. In some areas there are restrictions on storing and using old tires; be sure to check your local laws. I've also added different things to the dirt, such as dried herbs, diatomaceous earth, and wood ash. Because wood ash forms lye when mixed with rainwater, be sure to mix the ash well with the dirt.

DIY FODDER BOX

A fodder box is a great way to provide your chickens with fresh green forage during the off season or if you're raising them in a run and they aren't free-range. This fodder box will make a 2-by-4-foot rectangle. You can also opt to make a 4-by-4 square, but the chickens may have a hard time reaching the center and will be tempted to jump on the wire to reach it. A long, narrow rectangle is best.

WHAT YOU'LL NEED:

- Two 1-by-4-by-8-foot pieces of untreated wood: cedar, birch, oak, or pine would work; cedar is less prone to rot, and pine rots quicker than the other choices
- Saw
- Hammer or drill and 1½-inch nails or screws
- Fill dirt (2 cubic feet for 3 inches of soil)
- Fodder seed: buckwheat, rye, barley, wheatgrass, etc.
- One 4½-by-2½-foot piece chicken wire or 1-inch hardware cloth
- Staple gun and staples or wire tacks

WHAT TO DO:

1. Cut one of the 1-by-4-by-8 pieces in half. These sections will be your long (4-foot) sides.
2. Using the other 1-by-4-by-8, cut two 2-foot sections from it. These will be your short (2-foot) sides.
3. Assemble the frame using the nails or screws.
4. Add 3 inches of soil, but do not fill to the top of the frame. You don't want your chickens eating the seeds before they sprout.
5. Spread out the fodder seed on the soil and add a thin layer (¼ inch) of soil over top of the seeds.
6. Attach the wire tightly across the top and secure with staples or wire tacks.
7. Water the fodder daily and make sure the soil is moist until the fodder grows.
8. Reseed as needed.

THE GOOD, THE BAD, AND THE UGLY

I'm sure by now you've experienced some, if not all, of the behaviors I am going to describe in this section. I will share some tips on how to deal with chicken misbehavior and other flock-related heartbreak.

Raising chickens does indeed come with its share of ups and downs. Bringing home baby chicks for the first time, or even the tenth, is one of the best things in the world. Cute, soft, fluffy, *a-dor-able*! But the disappointment can begin almost immediately, with a chick who is under the weather, not eating or drinking despite your best efforts. Or your chickens are delivered in the mail, only for you to realize the box isn't chirping like it should be. It happens, and it's hard every single time.

Sometimes, rather than heartbreak, the roller coaster of chicken keeping causes frustration. Let's not forget the extra chickens most hatcheries ship. Those extras (because loss does happen when shipping livestock) are often cockerels, even when you've paid extra to only get pullets. Of course, you won't know the difference until it's too late and they start crowing and you've grown attached.

Speaking of growing, what about those ugly teen years? You know that stage between "aww, they're so cute" and fresh eggs? The stage when they start losing their cute, fluffy down and grow their big-kid feathers. They poop all over, seem to be mean to each other, and quite frankly stink. But wait, there's more! This is just the first couple of months of being a chicken owner.

PECKING ORDER

At the very beginning stages of life, chickens establish a pecking order. When they are only a few days old, they begin to display their climb for the position at the top. The pecking order, or social hierarchy, is the chicken way of deciding who is king and queen of the flock. The rank of royalty is not established through popular vote but rather by bullying one another into submission. Some chickens cry "uncle!" early and have no problem with being the low gal on the perch, but others are a little more stubborn and go back for a second, third, and even fourth butt-kicking.

Once the pecking order is established, you will have a hen who is the top among the ladies, a rooster who is the top among the gents, and a mac daddy who rules the play yard. Generally, the order works, and there is nothing you can, or should, do. If you try to intervene, they will go right back to the pecking order as soon as you place them together. However, if you see blood, it's time to play referee.

Don't let a bloody comb, face, or wattle frighten you; it will happen. However, chickens are omnivores and are attracted to the color red. When they see that color, they will peck. I've seen eyes pecked out and chickens almost getting pecked to death because one started and they all ganged up. Not a pretty sight.

WHEN YOU SEE BLOOD

When you see blood, there are a couple of measures you can take to ensure the safety of your flock. Remove the injured chicken and assess the injury. Call a vet if needed. Clean the wound and use a made-for-livestock antiseptic blue dye such as Blu-Kote to cover the wound. Chickens attack red, so using blue dye disguises the wound, giving it time to heal. Give your injured feathered friend some food, water, and probiotics such as yogurt. Keep the injured chicken separate from the flock if the wound needs time to heal.

THE SCHOOLYARD BULLY

Many times, there isn't much you can do when it comes to your flock establishing a pecking order. However, if you have an aggressive hen or rooster, there are things you can try. Establish a separate area that you can use for time-outs. This area should include all the amenities of home, including a perch, shelter, food, and water. Place overly aggressive chickens in this time-out pen to give them a chance to cool off.

Consider emasculating the bully. Chickens see you as a member of their flock. Show them all that you are the biggest, baddest one of the bunch: Grab the bully and carry them around in front of other members of their flock. Do this for 5 to 10 minutes at a time.

Distraction might work as well. Chickens are easily distracted by food and/or toys. Create some entertainment on the play yard by giving them all treats to eat or roll over some rotten logs for them to scour for bugs. Hopefully, this means they will spend less time and energy picking on one another.

CANNIBALISM

When chickens start pecking another chicken, especially if there is blood from an injury, they will not stop. Yes, they will eat other chickens given a chance. Therefore, it's important to remove any injured chickens from your flock and treat them. You can return the injured chicken once they've healed, but keep an eye out for further injuries.

HOW TO REMOVE A ROOSTER'S SPURS

A rooster uses his spurs to protect his flock and to battle other roosters, but sometimes he will use these spurs for evil and will need to be relieved of his weapons. If he is causing injuries to your flock, has attacked you or another human, or is injuring himself or having trouble walking, you may need to remove your rooster's spurs. Keep in mind, though, that removing a rooster's spurs leaves him more vulnerable; don't take the decision to remove his spurs lightly.

A rooster's spurs are made of keratin, just like your fingernails and hair. And, just like nails and hair, there is no blood flow in the spurs themselves, so this is not major surgery. There are a couple of different methods for spur removal, but I find this one the easiest. All you need is a washcloth, soapy water, a hot potato (cooked in the microwave and cut in half), and a pair of pliers. Have some kind of blood stop on hand just in case there is a little bleeding.

WHAT TO DO:

1. Catch the rooster and hold him upside down by his legs.

2. Using a washcloth, wash off his feet and spurs with warm soapy water.

3. Place a hot potato half on each spur. The heat will soften the keratin and make the spur easy to remove. Leave the potato on for three to five minutes.

4. Using the pliers, firmly grab the spur, but don't squeeze too tightly. Turn the spur clockwise; it will pop right off.

5. Repeat on the other side.

6. Apply blood stop if there is any bleeding, and return the rooster to his flock.

BROODING

A broody hen will want to lay on eggs to hatch them out (see page 66 in chapter 4). If you don't have fertilized eggs for her to sit on or if you don't want her to hatch baby chicks, you will have to help break her broody cycle or she will continue to sit on the eggs. You can block her access to the nesting boxes, remove the eggs a couple times a day so there is nothing to sit on, or try to place a frozen water bottle under her while she is in the nesting box, which will discourage her from sitting.

REDUCING STRESS

Now that you have some eggs in your basket, so to speak, it's time to help your flock be the absolute best they can be. Stress in chickens can result in reduced egg production, attacks in your flock, diminished health, or early death. Fortunately, there are things you can do to help reduce or eliminate stress for your chickens. Again, spend time with your flock to observe their behavior and physical condition so you know what they need. While observing your flock, keep an eye out for these signs of stress:

- Feather loss

- Reduced egg production

- Missing back feathers

- Weight loss

- Isolation

- Lack of activity

STRESSORS

If you observe signs of stress in your chickens, the next step will be to diagnose and remove the stressors. This list includes common stressors for chickens, along with tips to help reduce or eliminate these problems. Many of these stressors and solutions are covered in more detail in later chapters. Use this list as a quick, easy reference for when you notice stress in your flock, and then you can flip to those more detailed sections as needed.

Overcrowding. Chickens who are overcrowded will fight, will have a hard time getting enough food, and are likely to become stressed. Check out recommendations for coop and run upgrades in chapter 2.

Predation. Remember, safety from predators is a basic need of your flock. See chapter 3 for more information about predators and how to keep your chickens safe from specific threats.

Lack of food and/or water. Those lowest in the pecking order will be the last in the lunch line. Make sure to have multiple food and water stations so that everyone has a place to stop in for a bite.

Hen-to-rooster ratio is off. The average hen-to-rooster ratio is one rooster to every 5 to 10 hens. More than that will stress the hens and create infighting.

Change in environment. Moving chickens to a new area or taking them to a 4-H show or to the farmers' market will create stress. To make the process as calm as possible, follow the Tips for Moving Day in chapter 2 (see page 32). In addition, if you are planning on showing your chickens or taking them to markets to keep on display, practice handling them a lot, from when they are chicks through their adult years.

Weather. Change in daylight hours, heat, cold, and weather extremes will all stress your flock. Make sure you regularly maintain your coop and that the chickens have protection from the elements (see chapter 3).

Too much or too little light. Certain colors of light cause stress in chickens. A study published in the *Journal of Applied Poultry Research* showed that chickens thrive better when kept under LED lights as compared to fluorescent lights. Another study published in *Poultry Science* found that certain colors of light, such as bright white-blue, cause chickens stress, while soft whites or ambers help calm them.

New chickens or other livestock. No one likes the new kids on the block, especially the low chicken in the pecking order. Those chickens will see a new arrival as a chance to finally move on up from the bottom. See chapter 4 (page 76) for tips on introducing new chickens to the flock in a way that minimizes stress.

CHAPTER 2
UPGRADING THE COOP AND RUN

The way I see it, chicken coops fall into a couple of categories: adorable coops that are not really practical, affordable coops that will do for now, and coops that are practical for the long term.

I'm not sure which category your first coop falls into; our first coop was adorable but less than practical. After that first one, we also bought an affordable and "will do for now" coop before landing on our current coop, which is practical, meets our needs, and will continue to do so for many years to come.

This chapter will cover the changes, additions, and improvements you can make to your coop so you can have continued success with your chickens and help them reach their full potential. The first step is to assess your chicken coop or run. Is it meeting all your needs and all your flock's needs? If not, explore some of the simple changes I have suggested in this chapter. Small changes can make a big difference.

FEATHERING THE NEST

As you are assessing your chicken coop and run and exploring options for improvements, here are some basic principles to keep in mind. If you realize your coop could use a little help in one of these areas, take a look at the following sections, which offer ideas for improvements that might greatly upgrade your chickens' space.

- Coops are where the chickens roost, sleep, lay eggs, and escape from inclement weather and predators. Do they have everything they need to do those things?

- Include enough perch space in your coop to make sure there is room for everyone to hang out. If your flock looks crowded now that they are all grown or if you've introduced new birds to your flock, consider adding another perch or two to the coop.

- You need a coop that offers ventilation but isn't drafty, and you want the coop to be easy to access for cleaning and collecting eggs.

- A coop for average-size chickens should include 2 to 3 square feet of space per chicken, not including nesting boxes. If you are raising larger breeds, such as Jersey Giants or Cochins, you should have 4 to 5 square feet of space per chicken.

- Your coop should include one nesting box per four or five hens. There needs to be enough comfortable nesting boxes that are safe from predators and other nosy chickens so the hens can lay their eggs in peace. If you don't have enough nesting box space, you can get a couple of milk crates and add them to your coop for makeshift nesting boxes. Keeping in mind, of course, that you can have 50 nesting boxes and they'll *ALL* want to lay eggs in that one special nesting box.

- Runs should be at least 10 to 12 square feet per chicken, although most chicken keepers like to have 25 feet per chicken for happier chickens. The more space chickens have to roam, the better. If you're not able to free-range your chickens, perhaps you can build them a chicken tractor to provide them with new land to forage.

FLOOR COVERINGS

Changing the floor covering in your coop is a great way to address concerns about cleanliness, ease of access, or smell. I know this from experience. When we built our first coop, we built it with a wood floor. Even though we changed the bedding often, the wood started swelling and buckling from the liquid in the manure. This caused all kinds of problems. So we painted and sealed the wood, which then started to mold.

Finally, we added a scrap piece of linoleum flooring. Adding the linoleum was a lifesaver! We found that the linoleum was easy to clean and protected the wood flooring. Linoleum was a great water-resistant solution to our problem; other flooring options that work well in coops include concrete, tile, or even dirt.

EASIER CLEANING

Anyone who has ever cleaned out a chicken coop knows what a pain it can be. It is seriously one of my least-favorite farm chores. Coops are stinky, hard to clean, and an overall disgusting mess. I swear, judging by the amount of chicken manure that's around, you would think chickens consume their entire body weight in food every day. If you are looking for an easier, more efficient way to clean out your coop, trust me, you are not alone.

We finally decided to work smarter and not harder by installing a tarp under the perches in our coop. We placed two hooks under the top perch and attached the tarp through the grommets. Then we installed two more hooks under the bottom perch and attached the other end of the tarp. The tarp acts like a trap catchment for all the poop the chickens produce when they are on their perches—which is a *LOT*. When it's time to clean we just unhook the tarp, fold it in half, and remove it from the coop.

ELECTRICITY AND CLIMATE CONTROL

One of the later additions we made to our coops, which turned out to be a huge improvement, was installing an outdoor receptacle (aka an outdoor electrical outlet) near the coop. We used this power source for both a fan in the summer and a light in the winter. If you are interested in a similar upgrade, consult with or hire a professional electrician. Safety first!

We don't use heat lamps, as they have been known to cause many fires, but we have used a light with an incandescent light bulb during the cold nights. Incandescent light bulbs can produce 150 to 250 degrees Fahrenheit on their surface. Always use caution with lights and heaters with coops. Keep them free of dust, dander, and debris, which can catch fire. Make sure your lights or heat sources are well secured and that the chickens cannot reach them.

VENTILATION: WINDOWS AND FANS

As I mentioned in the checklist (see page 24), your coop must have adequate ventilation in both winter and summer. Not only does ventilation provide your chickens with fresh air, but it also helps prevent condensation and breathing problems associated with ammonia exposure. If you begin to see condensation on the ceiling of your coop, start to see mold developing inside the coop, or notice your chickens coughing, it's time for more ventilation.

If your coop doesn't have a window or doesn't have quite enough airflow, consider adding a window. Make sure you don't place the window too close to the perches, so the chickens don't get cold. Cutting a window is a relatively simple solution and will help a lot with ventilation. We successfully cut a window out of the side of our coop and decided to fit the opening with hardware cloth rather than glass so that there is always a nice airflow.

Even if you have great ventilation in your coop, the climate can still cause problems. Our summers were brutal near the beach in South Carolina, and our feathered friends were not happy about it. We had proper ventilation, but they were still too hot. To help our flock cool down, we installed a small box fan outside their window (on the outside of the coop), which gave them some much-needed respite from the brutal summer heat. There are a few things to keep in mind if you want to provide a fan for your chickens, too. Make sure to keep the fan motor clean, and angle the fan so that it is not blowing directly on the chickens.

GROW-OUT COOP OR TIME-OUT ZONE

If you're raising baby chicks and adding them to your existing flock, it's a good idea to have a smaller grow-out coop, which provides a place for them when they are between brooding chicks and the big coop. After they have grown their feathers and are too big for the brooder but are still too small to defend themselves from the big kids, a grow-out coop is a great asset. Consider buying a cheap premade coop online to use for this purpose. Young chickens will generally stay in this separate coop when they are from 8 to 16 weeks old.

When you have a sick chicken or a bully who needs an attitude adjustment, they need to be removed from the flock. The grow-out coop can double as a sick bay or a bully time-out coop. However, if you can't afford another coop or don't have the additional space, consider partitioning an area in your existing coop that can be completely blocked off from other chickens. We did this in one of our coops by adding a 3-foot-high wall on one side of the coop and building a separate access door. We covered the top of it with chicken wire so the chickens couldn't just jump in or out.

NESTING BOXES WITH ACCESS HATCH

Collecting eggs from the front of a chicken who is sitting on eggs is not a fun eggs-perience. Chickens don't like giving up their eggs, and you are well within attacking range—not to mention that disturbing them can reduce future production. There are many times we just want to check on our beloved hens without disturbing them—a task much easier to accomplish if you have an access panel in your coop.

Once we realized how troublesome it was to collect eggs from inside the coop, we decided to create an access panel from the outside of the coop by cutting the back of their nesting boxes off and adding a piano hinge and a hook and eye. Then all we had to do was open the panel and take a peek—no fuss, no muss, and no more fingers pecked by a defensive mama hen.

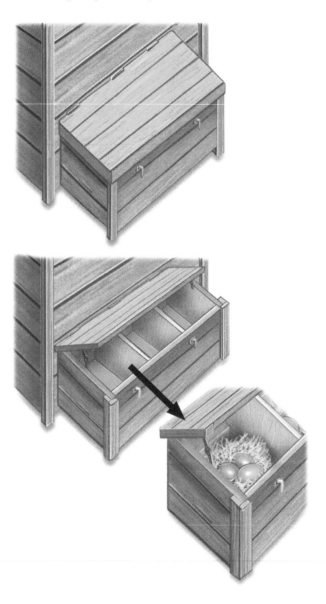

WEAR AND TEAR

Whether it is caused by children, renters, or chickens, wear and tear is a normal and expected part of life. Of course, some chickens—just like some people—are harder on their surroundings than others are, and some materials hold up better than others. This is why when I consider what's "affordable and will do for now," I also consider that coops made from cheaper materials don't last for very long under normal-ish conditions and will require a lot of TLC to maintain.

Of course, I speak from experience. Our "affordable" coop was less than a couple of months old when our goats decided it would be a fun toy to jump on; they completely dismantled it within a day. So that was that. We then moved on to a hand-built coop, though we soon encountered the aforementioned flooring issue. Long story short, no matter what kind of coop you have, you will have to perform some upkeep if you want it to last.

The building materials and roofing used for your coop will largely determine the maintenance you'll have to perform to keep it in top running order. With proper care, a good chicken coop can last decades, so if it is within your budget, it's wise to invest in hardy materials right from the start. Tin roofs require less maintenance than wood or shingle roofs. Plastic or metal walls require less maintenance than wood walls. Our current coop has a tin roof and wood walls and floor (covered with the previously mentioned linoleum), and our yearly maintenance checklist consists of the following—which is a good place to start if you are planning your annual maintenance for your coop.

- Deep cleaning the coop from top to bottom

- Sealing any new draft areas or cracks in the wood

- Adding a coat of paint or wood stain to the exterior

- Replacing any broken perches or those that are beyond cleaning

- Checking for mice and snakes and sealing any holes

- Tightening loose hinges on doors, nesting boxes, and fencing

- Securing any loose wiring

- Checking the roof for leaks and repairing as needed

MOVING THE PENTHOUSE

Unfortunately, there may come a time when you need to relocate your entire chicken coop. Thankfully, this is not a maintenance task that every chicken keeper encounters. It is a challenge and takes some planning, though, so it bears mentioning here. A few common reasons why you might have to move your coop include compliance with building codes, complaints from your neighbors, or if the land under your coop and run becomes over-worked or infested with parasites. (We will talk more about this last issue on page 93.)

Moving an established chicken coop is never a fun task. We've done this twice, and that is two times too many for my taste. The first time we were actually rehoming our chick-ens because we were moving out of state, so we hauled our 5-by-14-foot cedar-and-oak chicken coop and run two hours' drive away. The second time was when we moved to the moun-tains and the previous location of our coop was in a death trap (aka a holler), making our livestock sitting ducks for predators. We needed to relocate the coop for their safety.

TIPS FOR MOVING DAY

Moving is stressful for everyone. I have never met man nor beast who enjoys packing and moving. Here are some tips to reduce stress and help your flock on the big day.

Don't play tag. Avoid chasing chickens in the yard to pack them up for moving. Try to gather your flock during the night when they are roosting and sleeping to avoid added stress. If you use a red light (instead of a regular white light) to see in the coop, chances are they will be very easy to catch.

Prepare temporary housing. Try to have a suitable space for them to stay during the move, such as several large dog crates, a baby playpen with chicken wire across the top, or even the back of a truck with a camper shell.

Use soothing scents. Lavender has been shown to be calming for chickens (and humans). Try adding lavender to their coop or temporary housing.

Offer treats and water. Offering your flock some special treats, such as live mealworms or crickets, may be just the ticket for keeping them occupied during the move.

Keep them locked up. If you're moving your chickens to a new location and you plan to free-range, keep them locked up in their coop for three days and then in their run for two weeks. This will train them to recognize this is their new home and not to leave this new location.

CLEANING

Unfortunately, although we can teach chickens how to do math, we have yet to teach them how to clean their own house. Therefore, we must do it for them.

Some of the coop upgrades I suggested earlier in this chapter will greatly aid in the onerous task of cleaning your coop, such as creating a tarp poop catcher (see Easier Cleaning, page 25) or installing linoleum flooring for easier heavy-duty cleaning days (see page 25). Here are some other useful tips for keeping the coop nice and clean, which is imperative for maintaining a healthy flock.

Bedding. Keep the bedding in your coop fresh. Remember, eggs stay clean and pretty if your hens have fresh bedding in their nesting boxes. Thick bedding also absorbs manure better, and this helps reduce smell. There are many bedding choices you can use in your coop, each best suited for specific needs. Common bedding materials include hay, pine straw, pine shavings, hemp, shredded newspaper, and sand.

» We prefer to use hay because we always have it on hand and it's readily accessible. I use wood shavings (the large ones) in the brooder because it's easier for the baby chicks to walk on and doesn't keep the house smelling like hay. In my experience, pine straw isn't as absorbent as some of the other materials but would be fine to use in a run.

» We don't have hemp available locally, but it would be a good option if you do. Shredded newspaper (not the shiny ads but the black-and-white newsprint) is an affordable option if you have a local source. The task of shredding it can become tedious over time if you don't have a paper shredder, though.

» Sand has long been debated among chicken owners. Some argue that it's the best thing since sliced bread; others say it harbors too much bacteria because you can't clean it. I don't have a source near me, so I don't have a dog in this fight. It will have to be a personal decision whether to use sand. Do your research and weigh the pros and cons.

The right tools for the job. Attach a hook to the wall in the chicken coop and keep a dust brush with a long handle to get down any cobwebs. I have found that a good pair of rubber gloves, a dust mask, a stiff bristle brush, a wide shovel, a wheelbarrow, and a hoe are the best tools for cleaning the chicken coop.

Elbow grease. Skip harmful cleaning chemicals in the chicken coop, as they can be toxic to chickens. We clean with straight cleaning-grade vinegar and good old-fashioned elbow grease.

CHICKEN POOP

Anyone who's raised chickens for any length of time has a chicken poop story. If not, here are some little words of wisdom: There is no such thing as going out to check on the chickens really quick in your dress shoes and not getting poop on them. Do yourself a favor and take the time to slide on some chore boots.

Let's get serious about poop. Take a moment to get all the poop jokes out of your system because we're about to get down and dirty talking about number two. Chicken poop can contain some pretty nasty stuff for us humans, including serious critters like *E. coli, salmonella,* and *cryptosporidium.* Using proper care when being exposed to chicken manure and cleaning their coop is essential to your health. I cannot stress this enough. Don't become complacent because you've raised chickens, your mama raised chickens, and ain't nobody ever got sick from chicken poop. It's a real thing and can make you very sick.

When coming in contact with chicken poop and cleaning the coop, wear gloves, use a dust mask, make sure you are in a well-ventilated area (don't close the coop doors while you're inside), and use protective eyewear.

In addition, burning chicken poop can cause toxic ash that is very harmful to inhale. Make sure to dispose of the manure in a compost pile and do not burn it. Dispose of chicken manure by adding it to the compost bin and adding three parts leaves, hay, straw, bedding, etc., to one part chicken manure. Allow chicken manure to decompose for at least 120 days before using it in the garden.

MAINTAINING THE RUN

When you were just starting out and had a brand-new run for your chickens, I'm willing to bet it looked great. Chicken runs start out dry and smelling like earth with fresh flooring, toys that are shiny and bright, clean perches.

One week after owning chickens, however, the run looks quite different. It is muddy and desolate with toys that are dull and dirty. Any plants in the vicinity have been eaten, and perches are now completely decorated with chicken poop.

Your chickens' run, just like the coop, needs to be cleaned and maintained to keep your chickens happy and healthy. Your run is where your chickens will most likely spend 99 percent of their waking hours. This is where they will forage for food, scratch, bathe, hang out in the sun, and mate. Here are a few ideas for keeping your run in top shape and best practices for regular maintenance.

WEEKLY RUN CHORES

Chickens who are confined to a specific area for prolonged periods of time will tend to overwork the land. This means they will peck all the goodies out of the soil they are provided with. This is one of the reasons why many chicken keepers choose to build a chicken tractor.

Some farmers implement rotational grazing: They move their flock to a specific area of land for 30 days and then continue to move them every 30 days, usually in a clockwise pattern. They do this so the land doesn't get overworked and the parasites that live in the soil don't have a chance to gain in numbers. The chickens continue to get fresh forage, the land gets tilled and fertilized, and everyone is happy.

Unfortunately, this is not a viable option for many backyard chicken keepers. Therefore, it is important to follow good chicken run maintenance procedures. This checklist is a good start for chores that should be performed weekly.

- Remove manure and soiled bedding/flooring.

- Keep the run floor dry.

- Fill holes: Chickens love to scratch and dig holes while dust bathing and looking for food. These holes in the yard and walking paths can be dangerous for us humans and become a tripping hazard. Best to fill them in as needed.

- Add fresh bedding/flooring.

- Clean perches, feeders, and toys with vinegar and water.

- Offer a well-balanced diet, including fodder, crushed oyster shells, insects, grit, and various produce.

MUDDY AND WET RUN FLOOR

Run flooring that is constantly too wet can cause foot problems in chickens, promote parasite loads, cause food to spoil, create mold, and is just plain nasty. Chickens and standing water do not mix. I have encountered this issue myself. One season it rained five out of seven days a week for three months, and it was nearly impossible to keep our chicken run dry. We used the following techniques, which you can try if you ever find your chicken run muddy and soaked.

- Dig trenches to divert the water away from the run.

- Wrap a tarp around three sides of the run to keep the rain out while still allowing for airflow.

- Remove wet flooring and replace it frequently with dry straw.

- Add wood chips to the ground or flooring to aid with drainage.

- For a longer-term project, consider installing a roof over the run instead of framed wire.

In addition to these suggestions, you can add gravel or concrete to your run floor for a more permanent solution to consistent mud and water issues. If you're using concrete, I would recommend adding pine shavings to the floor to absorb the manure and add cushion for the chickens' feet.

RUN ADDITIONS

Chickens can get bored, and bored chickens can become depressed or instigate fights. Luckily, you don't have to dress like a clown and make balloon animals to keep your chickens entertained. Just make a few additions to your run, and they will be the ones entertaining you. Here are a few fun suggestions for you to try—nothing outrageous, just simple additions that can help bring your flock to the next level in reaching their full potential.

Fodder box. As we know, chickens love to graze and will be on the constant hunt for fresh yummies to eat. Frame a 2-by-4-foot section of earth with some 1-by-4-inch lumber, fill your sectioned-off area with dirt, sprinkle with fodder or grass seeds, cover with chicken wire, and you have a green buffet for your chickens. See page 12 for detailed instructions. Depending on the size of your run, you may also want to consider planting some bushes or a dwarf tree.

Fun toys and treats. Chickens are curious and playful. Be creative with fun activities to add to your run. You may want to include a xylophone or a child's piano. Our chickens love walking in the small plastic kiddie pool that we set out for them in the summer. If you don't want to add water to your pool, consider adding dirt and a bunch of worms for a great scratching feast.

PVC feeder. Use a 4-inch-diameter PVC pipe to make an oyster shell feeder. Sections about 18 inches long work well for this project. To one end of the 18-inch section, add a 4-inch PVC elbow fitting and secure with pipe glue. In our coop, we use wire to attach the PVC feeder to an inside wall. We fill the pipe with crushed oyster shells, and the chickens eat them as they wish.

FREE-RANGE CHICKENS

Free-range means having access to the outdoors without being confined. I've had personal experience with raising chickens both in a run and free-range, and I can confidently say that they both have their pros and cons. If you're considering letting your flock loose to the great outdoors, there are some things you may want to consider. As a chicken owner, you will have to weigh the pros and cons and decide what is best for you and your flock. There isn't going to be one answer that is the best for every situation and every chicken keeper. The truth is, you can raise a happy, healthy flock either way.

FREE-RANGE PROS

Happy, fit chickens: The more space chickens have to roam, the happier they are and the more physically fit they will be.

Balanced diet and reduced feed cost: The more chickens forage for their own food, the less chicken feed they need. They will also eat a variety of things, providing a more balanced diet.

Less infighting: When chickens aren't confined, they tend not to fight as much. If they do run into a bully, they can escape more easily.

Pest control and a fertilized yard: The benefit of chickens pooping everywhere is that it helps fertilize your yard. Hungry chickens also love to eat spiders, ticks, worms, and bugs.

Less boredom and depression: No need to create boredom busters when the chickens have a field to scratch in, a tree to perch in, or leaves they can dig under for worms. Free-range chickens will also make their own dust baths, no help needed.

FREE-RANGE CONS

Predators: If your property is fenced in and you have livestock guardians, you may have less to worry about. But even then, flying predators are a concern.

No respect for property lines: You will most likely be responsible for damage that your chickens cause, which might include digging up your neighbor's prized flower bed.

Freedom to stay away: They may leave and never come back: When chickens roam off your property, they may think the grass is greener on the other side.

Poop everywhere: On your steps, on your porch, on the handrails . . .

Breeding specific breeds is difficult if you free-range, as it is tough to control reproduction. An Easter Egger rooster may mate with your Heritage Breed hen, creating a crossbreed baby chick.

CHAPTER 3

PROTECTING AGAINST WEATHER AND PREDATORS

While I can't claim that I have seen it all, I've certainly experienced many kinds of extreme weather, from hurricanes and flooding to ice and snowstorms. When I first began keeping chickens, we lived at the beach with extreme heat. Now we live in the mountains, where we encounter debilitating snowstorms.

In addition to extreme weather, my flock and I have also had to deal with many wildlife predators, including raccoons, bobcats, coyotes, eagles, hawks, opossums, foxes, snakes, and bears. We live close to the national forest; predators are always a concern.

In this chapter, I'll share my experiences with you as we discuss how to keep your livestock safe from both Mother Nature and wild beasts.

SHORING UP FOR THE SEASONS

Your flock will have different requirements throughout the seasons depending on where you live. You may have harsh winters but mild summers. Or maybe you live where the summers are brutal but the winters are calm. Use the information in the sections here as a starting point and adjust as needed to suit your climate.

Of course, with more than 500 chicken breeds—each with different traits—some chickens are well suited for tropical climates while others thrive in colder temperatures. Do your research to find the breeds that do best in your specific climate before adding more chickens to your flock.

LIVE THINGS FIRST

We have a rule at our homestead: Live Things First. This means that no matter what chores we have on our plates, the chores that address the needs of living things are top priority, whether those living creatures have two legs or four. This is especially true when preparing for pending bad weather. This unwritten rule helps us stay focused when we are worried or stressed or when we have a lot of tasks that need to be accomplished; I hope that it will help you, too.

SPRING

Often, spring is cold, wet, and muddy with high winds. The days become longer, and most people choose this season to bring home new baby chicks. For more-established chickens, this is the time of year to molt and lose old feathers. Chickens generally molt twice a year, in the spring and the fall. You can read more about what molt is and how to help your chickens through it on page 88, but it's important to know that during molting time, your chickens are vulnerable and need extra protection from the elements, such as wind, rain, and cold.

At my house, springtime is also the time for a spring cleaning and getting ready for the upcoming warm season. For us, this means deeply cleaning the chicken coop, nesting boxes, and run. Your chickens need a clean and safe living environment to help keep them healthy. Dampness, dust, drafts, exposed nails, piled manure filled with ammonia, and parasites that can live in the bedding all pose health risks for your flock. Performing a good spring cleaning and coop maintenance will aid in their overall health and happiness. Find tips for your spring clean on page 33.

Rain. Perhaps you have heard the saying "Madder than a wet hen." Chickens don't like to frolic in the rain. Of course, they love foraging for all the worms that a good rain produces, but they are not fans of getting wet. During the heavy spring rains, chickens need shelter to escape the elements. They also need to be able to dry off before the temperatures dip at night. Their food should be placed out of the rain, even if that means moving it temporarily.

> » If you can't provide natural shelter such as trees or shrubs that your flock can seek cover under, try hanging tarps, extending the roof on their coop, or placing a sheet of tin over their run.

» Humidity from rain can cause food to mold, which in turn can cause health and respiratory issues. If your chickens' food gets rained on or becomes damp due to extreme humidity, be sure to clean out the feeders, washing them with cleaning vinegar and drying them completely before refilling.

Flooding. In 2015 we had a 1,000-year flood in South Carolina. Homes, farms, and businesses were destroyed. Our property was flooded for a week, and it was all we could do to take care of our human responsibilities, not to mention our chickens. We witnessed livestock on roofs trying to survive. It was a horrific experience and reminded me of the importance of never leaving a flock to fend for themselves in extreme weather. Chickens will not swim or fly to safety.

» During a flooding situation like the one we faced in 2015, it's important to have a way to transport your flock, like a large dog crate or two. If you live in an area prone to flooding, take some time now to scope out higher ground where you can move your flock if the waters start to rise. In our situation, our entire yard was flooded, but the coop itself was a couple of feet above water, so we were able to safely keep our flock locked in their coop until the waters receded. During this time, we made sure they had food, fresh water, and dry bedding. I also tried to provide treats to keep them from feeling bored or from starting fights with one another.

» Wet, contaminated soil and the ensuing mold can be problematic for chickens and other livestock. When the waters recede after a flood, remove the top couple inches of soil in their run, if possible. If this is not possible, add fresh soil or compost. When we were recovering from our flood, we purchased a liquid treatment of beneficial microbes to treat the soil. This helped naturally combat the bacteria and clean up soil that was contaminated by the flood. We also added a couple inches of mulch that we received from all the felled trees. If your community experiences a flood, keep your eyes open for similar resources.

» After flooding, continue to perform wellness checks on your flock, especially inspecting their feet. Much like when you sit in the bathtub for too long and your skin gets soft and wrinkly, chickens can get soggy feet if they are in damp conditions for too long. This can lead to infection or foot rot.

SUMMER

Ahh, the dog days of summer. Summer means longer days of sunshine, hot temperatures, increased humidity or dryness, and sometimes drought. It's also the beginning of hurricane season (that's always fun). I don't miss evacuating every year due to approaching hurricanes, and you have my sympathy if this is something you must deal with.

Most likely the biggest issue for your flock in summer is the heat. Heat can cause stress and even death. You may have noticed that chickens also quit laying eggs if the temperatures are too hot. While I don't suggest installing a luxurious air conditioner in the chicken coop, there are a few things you can do to help support your flock's happiness and health during the heat of summer. Here are some suggestions for cooling your feathered friends.

Fans. As discussed in chapter 2 (see page 27), installing a window fan in the coop can help promote air circulation and cool things down. We used this technique when we lived at the beach, where temperatures exceeded 100 degrees Fahrenheit many days in a row. Whether or not you install a fan, make sure your coop has good ventilation and airflow. If you notice condensation on your coop roof, mold on the coop walls, or your chickens cough a lot, you need to add ventilation.

> » Don't confuse ventilation with drafts, which can cause problems of their own. A drafty coop is one where air blows right through and across your chickens. Two windows located on opposite walls, directly across from each other, would create drafts. However, a window on one wall and a vent at the top of an adjoining wall would add ventilation.

Shady perches. Provide shade for your flock by using tarps, tin sheet, trees, or shrubs; just make sure they have plenty of places to get out of the sun. Adding some perches to shady spots around your yard or chicken run helps keep them off the hot soil. In the past, we have used old wood sawhorses to great success; they are easy to move, and the chickens like perching on them.

Fresh water and electrolytes. Make sure your chickens have plenty of fresh water daily—twice a day is better. If it is very hot, consider placing a few gallon buckets filled with water around their run or yard.

> » Just as we like to enjoy a cold sports drink on a hot summer day, your chickens will appreciate electrolyte packets added to their water during the summer months. This supports the health of your flock by helping their bodies rehydrate. You can purchase electrolyte packets at any farm store that sells chicken feed.

Wading pool. A hard plastic kiddie pool filled with a couple inches of water is a great way for your chickens to cool off. Adding a couple grapes that they can chase around in the pool offers some fun time and snacks as well.

Ice treats. Give the chickens ice treats during the summer. Buy some cheap ice cube trays and fill them with fruit, worms, and crickets; then add water and freeze. They will love them!

FALL

Fall is when the chickens start to lay eggs again after going on strike in the summer heat. It's also when they begin to molt again (see page 88). The temperature starts dropping, the days become shorter, and the winds pick up. In some locations, you might even deal with frost in the fall.

Fall is the time you want to prepare your chicken coop for the winter months. During the fall, we usually begin to add cracked corn to their diet as well. Because cracked corn is harder for the chickens to digest, it helps increase their body temperature when they eat it. It also provides some extra calories for the colder months.

Even though the temperature will drop during fall and winter, it is still incredibly important to have ventilation in your chicken coop. The moisture from manure and body heat will create condensation. Without ventilation, this condensation can cause respiratory problems. Try the following tricks to protect your flock from the cold without blocking the ventilation in the coop.

Weatherize the coop. Use plastic, house wrap, or even hay bales around the coop to protect it from the wind, cold, or snow. Block all drafts in the coop by using plastic, caulk, or hay. Heat rises, so consider adding insulation to the ceiling to help prevent the heat from escaping.

Lighting. Add lighting to help encourage egg production or to bring in a little added heat. Avoid heat lamps, as they are a fire risk. A well-insulated coop, free from drafts, with plenty of bedding and clean light bulbs is all that you need for heat in most cases.

Cover. In the fall, trees and plants become bare, thus potentially removing your flock's camouflage protection from predators. Make sure your chickens have something to hide under when danger is near. Bushes, dog crates, or even wood planks leaning up against the building are good hiding places for the cooler months. Our chickens hide in and behind everything, even rain barrels.

WINTER

Our flock does not like the white stuff. As a matter of fact, I'm pretty sure some of them cussed me out the last time it snowed when they wanted to play in the yard. The bugs disappear, and so does your chickens' favorite pastime: scratching in the dirt.

In winters past, you may have noticed that your flock refused to go outside and play in the snow. Instead, they just stay in the coop until Mother Nature gives them the weather they want. If this is the case with your flock, you'll want to follow the same advice that I provided for floods (see page 46). Keep fresh bedding in their coop, provide clean, fresh food and water, and add some boredom busters so they stay happy and healthy. Here are a few tips and tricks to help meet your flock's winter needs.

Water. One of the main issues with winter weather is freezing water. Your chickens can get dehydrated in the winter just as easily as they can in the summer. When the temperature drops below freezing, change your flock's water several times a day to prevent it from turning to solid ice. You may also want to consider adding a water warmer (you'll find them at feed stores) to keep their water from freezing. If you can't add an electric warmer in their water dish, try adding hay or straw around their waterer to help insulate the container and keep the water from freezing.

Feed. Weather is never predictable, especially in winter. Always make sure you have at least a couple weeks' worth of chicken feed stocked up. You never know when you'll be snowed in and not able to get to the feed store.

Frostbite. In the cold, chickens risk frostbite. Chickens with large combs are more prone to frostbite than chicken breeds with smaller combs, such as the Pea Comb. If you have chickens with large, single combs and you're expecting temperatures below freezing, try coating their combs with coconut oil or lanolin. The oil will help protect their sensitive skin against frostbite.

> » Another frostbite concern for chickens is their feet. When chickens roost in the cold, they lower their chest over their feet to keep them warm and protected. Perches that are too small in diameter force the chickens to wrap their toes around the perch. When this happens, they can't protect their toes with their chest feathers, thus making them more susceptible to frostbite. To help prevent this, install perches that are at least 2 inches in diameter or use flat perches that allow the chickens to place their entire foot on the perch.

Activity. No one likes to crawl out of their nice warm bed on a cold winter day, and chickens are no exception. That said, it is important for your flock's health and happiness that they get outside to move and frolic when the weather permits. Sometimes they might need a nudge to get some fresh air and outdoor time. Encourage activity by tossing out some cracked corn or other treats to get them outside for a little bit.

PREDATOR PRECAUTIONS AND PROTECTIONS

When we lived at the beach and had a tiny coastal homestead, we rarely dealt with predator problems other than the occasional opossum or snake. Now that we live near the Smoky Mountain National Park, the entire wildlife division wants to make a meal out of our flock! So I speak from personal experience when I say that even with the best anti-predation measures in place, life still happens. As chicken keepers, we can do our best to protect our flocks from predators by avoiding becoming complacent or letting our guard down.

Let's face it, chicken tastes good—even to other chickens. There is a reason your feathered friends may have so many animals wanting to eat them. If you have experience with predators, you know how disheartening it can be when one of your chickens becomes a meal.

A few years back, we were coming home from my daughter's birthday celebration. The first thing we saw when we pulled in our driveway was a couple of feathers. Then more feathers. Then the body of my favorite rooster, minus the head. Then more dead bodies. The total body count for that horrific day was over 20. This happened in broad daylight, and we had been gone from the house for less than three hours. My daughter's special day was ruined, and we lost over half of our flock.

Losing your flock to predators may affect you on many different levels. Not only are they your companions and a source of fresh eggs, but they are also a huge investment of your time and money. When we lost our flock, it took over half a year to start over. Hopefully the following sections will help you prevent such an incident with your own flock or to recover should the worst happen.

WHODUNIT? IDENTIFYING THE CULPRIT

After the devastation of losing one, or even all, of your birds to predators, the first thing you want to figure out is who made a meal of your flock. Identifying the culprit can sometimes help you prevent future attacks. When you understand what you're dealing with, it will give you clues about how to stop them.

Each predator will leave a different sign, though sometimes the sign is no sign at all. For instance, we had an eagle swoop down out of the sky and grab one of our hens who was foraging in the yard. No tracks, no feathers, just one moment we had a hen frolicking in the yard eating worms and the next moment she was gone.

Other predators will leave signs such as tracks, fur, or even parts of the chicken that will give you clues as to what you're dealing with. Following is a list of predators that may attack your flock and telltale signs they may leave behind. Of course, this isn't a complete list, and predators vary depending on where you live. I encourage you to use this list as a launching point for more research.

Bears won't attack during hibernation. (They are typically inactive from late fall through early spring.) In the case of a bear attack, the coop and/or fence will be damaged, if not completely destroyed.

Bobcats attack day or night and will cause damage to the coop or fence.

Cats will also attack day or night. If a domestic cat has been in with your chickens, you will see lots of feathers scattered and pieces of the chickens left behind.

Coyotes only attack at night. They will haul off the whole chicken.

Dogs are active both day and night. Signs of a domestic dog invasion include mauled chickens, either intact or in parts, as well as wet feathers.

Eagles attack during the day and usually leave no visible signs.

Fishers are a kind of weasel that attack early in the morning and in the evening. They will bite the rear off the chicken and pull the entrails out.

Foxes will attack day or night. Foxes will typically haul off the whole chicken and kill more chickens than they can eat. They will also bury their kill, so if you find buried dead chickens, your culprit is a fox.

Hawks, like eagles, attack during the day and leave no trace. The exception is that you may find a body off at a distance with the side eaten out.

Humans have unfortunately been known to steal chickens for their own use or to kill chickens out of malice. Of course, humans are capable of attacking anytime and may leave a variety of traces, depending on their motives.

Minks attack in the early morning or in the evening. They will often leave the body and just drink the blood.

Opossums are active at night. They will eat eggs and only parts of the chicken, leaving other parts behind.

Owls, as you might imagine, attack at night. Owls often eat the head and neck and leave the body.

Raccoons attack at night and will remove the head from their kill.

Rats can attack your flock at any time but are more active at night. Traces of rat invasion include broken eggs or empty shells, as well as missing chicks.

Skunks attack at night and will leave their telltale odor behind. After a skunk attack, you will also notice missing eggs as well as the stomach and entrails missing from chicken bodies.

Snakes can attack both day and night. Baby chicks and eggs will be missing.

Weasels hunt in the early morning or at night. They kill for sport and will leave the whole body.

As painful as it is, when you experience a predator attack on your flock, the more quickly you investigate the scene, the more quickly you can work to protect the remaining chickens. In my experience, if a predator came once, they will come again. You need to work quickly to secure your flock before the predator returns. Take the following steps to investigate the scene.

- Before you ever deal with a predator attack, familiarize yourself with the wildlife in your area.

- Identify the damage to your flock and cross-reference it with the predator list on pages 54–56, consulting additional resources if needed.

- Check for places of entry in your coop, run, and fence.

- Look for tracks or scat.

- Check for any claw marks or digging around the perimeter of the coop and run.

POINTS OF ACCESS

If your flock has been attacked, it's time to look for possible entry points into your coop.

- Check all windows and vents for openings or cracks.
- Remove bedding off the coop floor and make sure there are no holes, cracks, or signs of rodents.
- Check walls for openings, including the space above and below the coop door.
- Fill any holes in the run and around the outside perimeter.
- Check the nesting boxes and make sure the lid or hatch closes snugly.
- Look in all the corners, under shelves, and above door and window casings. Snakes love to hide there.
- See if any of the wire has been spread open or if there are any breaks in the wire. Remember, predators can enter holes as small as 1 inch.

Some predators will reach in through the wire of your run and try to pull the chicken's head through the wire. You can deter this by using small hardware cloth and by planting spiky plants or shrubs around your chicken coop. Plants that have spikes, like Spanish daggers, cacti, and century plants, are all great deterrents.

PREDATOR PREVENTION

Even if you dedicate lots of time and energy to protecting your flock, life can still happen. However, you can sleep better knowing you did all you could instead of living with regret and wishing you had done more. The following are techniques and tips that I have used to protect my flock from predation.

Rooster. A good rooster will give his life defending his flock. You will also be able to hear if a rooster is defending his flock—the sounds are much like cockfighting.

Livestock guardian. A good livestock guardian (LG) animal is worth their weight in gold. LGs can be donkeys, dogs (only specific breeds), guinea fowl, geese, or llamas. Each LG is trained differently and protects the flock or herd in a different way. Most LGs are raised with the livestock they are to protect, and they are not necessarily pets but are working a full-time job. We have two livestock guardian dogs who live with our flock and goat herd. They chase off any would-be predators and even help keep the flock in line when they see fighting. Our guineas will sound their alarms (their voices) when they see something that doesn't belong.

Motion-sensitive lights. These will turn on when they detect motion and may help deter nighttime predators.

Radio. The sounds of a radio (tuned to human voices) may make potential predators think there are humans around, thus preventing them from approaching.

Trail/game cams. They can't stop a predator, but they can help you properly identify one. If your predators are human, you can take footage from your trail cam to the authorities.

Hardware cloth. Chicken wire is useless in protecting your flock. Use hardware cloth or welded wire no bigger than ½ inch throughout your chicken coop and run.

Camouflage tarp or netting. Hang it above your chicken run to hide them from flying predators and to prevent aerial attacks.

Foliage. Trees, shrubs, and plants are all things your chickens can hide in and under when predators are a threat.

Concrete or buried wire. Adding concrete around the perimeter of your coop protects your flock against prey that will dig under the walls or fence. If you can't install concrete, dig a trench around your coop and run and add wire to the side of your coop at least 1 foot down into the ground.

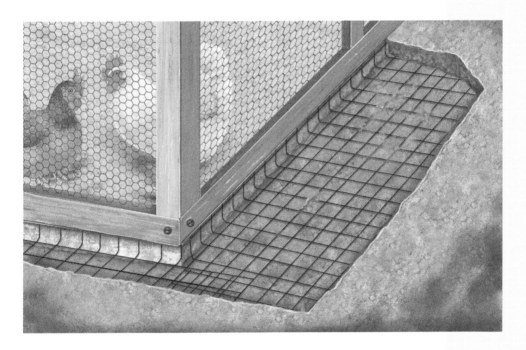

Lock them up. We've always made a habit of locking up our flock at night. Then we secure the door with a sturdy lock. Simple closures don't always work; predators are smart, and some have been known to open doors.

Avoid cracks and holes. Do a thorough inspection of your coop. Some predators can enter through a hole as small as 1 inch.

Fencing. A good fence will help protect against nonflying and climbing predators. It also helps keep your chickens from wandering off. Six-foot-high fencing is ideal.

HIGH-ALERT TIMES

While attacks can happen anytime, day or night, and in any season, there are times when they may be more common. These times include fall, before hibernation season, when animals that hibernate are looking to store food for the winter. Also be on high alert in the spring, when predators are working to feed their new babies. Hunting season can also be dangerous, when hunters run dogs that do not respect property lines. And finally, if there is a lack of food for wildlife (such as during times of drought or other severe weather), predators will move closer to humans to find a food source.

WHEN YOUR CHICKENS SOUND THE ALARM

After your flock is established and you've spent some time with them, you'll learn to recognize all their unique sounds—like the egg song, the "I'm hungry" sound, roosters fighting, mating sounds, and more.

A predator sound is no regular chicken sound. When a predator comes calling, the flock is either all in a commotion or completely quiet. If you hear a lot of ruckus coming from the henhouse, it's time to grab your shovel and go inspect the situation. Sometimes the chickens will circle and trap a smaller predator, like a snake or a rat. If you observe all your flock huddled together, chances are they are surrounding something that doesn't belong.

ELECTRIC FENCING PROS AND CONS

An electric fence can help keep your chickens in and predators out . . . sometimes. Much like all other predator defense preparations, nothing is a guarantee. From my experience, electric netting works best for poultry compared with single-strand electric fencing. Chickens seem to be able to walk right through a high-tensile wire fence.

PROS

Electric fencing protects your flock from predators, as an electric shock is enough to scare most predators away. If they are persistent, chances are you will hear them yelping through the fence.

The electric poultry netting is easy to move, and you can section off your yard to rotate your flock. Furthermore, electric fencing is not permanent, so you won't need building permits to set it up.

Electric fencing, like regular fencing, keeps your chickens contained where you want them to be.

CONS

An electric fence will not differentiate between predators and people. Be sure to talk to your children and neighbors about the presence of electric fencing on your property.

In addition to the original installation costs, electric fencing will add to your power bill.

Although electric netting is not as expensive as installing a 6-foot-high wood fence, it is a little pricey. Fully consider your decision before pressing the buy button.

CHAPTER 4
EXPANDING YOUR FLOCK

After you feel confident about caring for your flock, it's time to consider expanding to secure a sustainable flow of chickens and eggs. Let's face it—the hatchery catalog is better than the old Sears, Roebuck, and Co. one from when I was a kid. Keep in mind that while it's always fun to look at all the different breeds of chickens, it isn't necessarily cost-effective to buy chicks from a hatchery and pay for shipping and delivery. In this chapter, I'll cover all the ins and outs of raising your own generations of baby chicks.

A ROOSTER IN THE HENHOUSE

By now, I assume you already know that you don't need a rooster to get fresh eggs daily. However, if you don't have a rooster and you've been waiting for your eggs to hatch, we need to have a little chat about where babies come from. To get right to the point, hens by themselves lay unfertile eggs. Rooster + hen = fertile eggs and baby chicks.

If you want fertile eggs, you'll need a rooster. The suggested rooster-to-hen ratio is from one to five to one to ten. This means that for every 5 to 10 hens you have, you need one rooster. In my own flock, I have found a happy medium by keeping a one-to-eight ratio. With those numbers, my hens are content and I don't have too many cockfights.

These numbers might seem strange (one guy for eight girls!?), but you'd be surprised what one rooster can accomplish. You've heard the phrase "breed like rabbits." Well, I would put my dollar on a motivated rooster over a rabbit any day. A motivated rooster can breed 10 to 30 times per day! I can't imagine when they have time to eat and protect the flock.

Unfortunately, getting one rooster for every 5 to 10 hens is harder than it sounds. When hatching chickens or even ordering baby chicks from a hatchery, the chances of you getting a rooster when you only want hens is 50 percent. Unless of course you order pullets. But even then, they usually send extra birds with your order (which always end up being roosters, at least in my personal experience). In the last batch of eggs I hatched out, we had five roosters and only two hens. The odds were against me.

WHAT TO DO WITH EXTRA ROOS

Having too many roosters in a flock can cause serious issues, including cockfights, aggressive roosters, stressed hens, hens with naked backs (the roosters pluck their feathers), roosters who won't mate, lonely or ostracized roosters, and hens who won't lay eggs.

Sooner or later, if you raise chickens for any number of years, you're going to end up with an extra rooster or two or, in my case, five. So what do you do with them? You might be tempted to keep the extra roosters. You might be thinking, like I did, "If I raise them with love, handle them, care for them, and call them George, I will be different than all the chicken keepers before me." Not to mention roosters are more visually stunning than hens, with their beautiful plumage, wattles, and combs. It's okay; I don't blame you for being tempted. Unfortunately, every single time I've held on to extra roos, I have experienced one, if not all, of the problems I just mentioned.

Here are some options to consider if you find that you have too many roosters.

Try my failed method in an attempt to have one big happy family and keep all the roosters. (This is really not recommended.)

Contact a local 4-H, FFA, or extension office and see if they would like a rooster.

Contact your local feed store and see if you can advertise to rehome your rooster.

Attend a livestock auction to sell your surplus rooster(s).

Contact a local farm and inquire if they would like a rooster.

Place an ad on a local sales website like Craigslist.

Order more pullets to balance the hen-to-rooster ratio.

Process the bird for meat.

The problem of too many roosters is one that you want to consider before you start breeding chickens or hatching eggs. Have a plan in place so you know what to do when you have one too many roosters crowing at dawn.

ROMANCE IN THE HENHOUSE

Roosters start showing the desire to mate in their "teens," usually around 16 weeks. They try to woo their mates in various ways, from making subtle noises to pointing out the best food to swaying their wattles. Generally, the rooster at the top of the pecking order will have his pick of the ladies.

When a suitor finds his mate(s), you will witness something that looks like a rooster attacking a hen. He will generally grab the back of her neck with his beak, mount her back, spread his wings a little, and get down to business. Then he will hop off and get ready for the next hen.

Once mated, chickens can store viable sperm for up to two weeks. There is a good chance that all the eggs a hen lays for up to two weeks after mating are fertile. Of course, this isn't an exact science.

BROODY HENS AND BUYING EGGS

What can you do if you don't have a rooster stud muffin? The answer is a broody hen. A broody hen is a hen who is desperate to become a mama. She has great survival instincts and wants to raise future generations. A broody hen is worth her weight in gold. If you have a good hen who likes to go broody, you can keep her past her laying years to help hatch out eggs. "Hatching out" describes the process of a hen sitting on and incubating eggs to hatch baby chicks. An average-size chicken (not a bantam breed) can successfully hatch out a dozen eggs in a single clutch, give or take a few. A larger chicken breed, such as a Cochin, could hatch up to 15 or more.

Even if you don't have a rooster, your broody hen can still hatch out baby chicks. If you don't have a rooster and you want to have your broody chickens hatch out eggs, you can contact a local farm and inquire about purchasing fertile eggs from them.

Some hatcheries sell fertile eggs as well, at a fraction of the cost of buying baby chicks.

Consider contacting a local chicken keeper, too. We keep our roosters with our hens all the time, and after witnessing our roosters' daily activity, I can pretty much guarantee all the eggs we collect are fertile. We collect eggs daily (unless we want to hatch eggs), and I am more than happy to gift my fertile chicken eggs to people who want to hatch them out. Many other chicken keepers feel the same way.

However, if you don't have a rooster because of local laws, remember that any egg you hatch has a 50-50 chance of being a fellow. To prepare for potential problems and to stave off potential heartbreak, make a plan about what you might do with extra roos before you start hatching chickens. While breeders and hatcheries can sex day-old chicks, it's impossible to determine the sex of a chicken before it's hatched.

TO BREED OR NOT TO BREED

As a backyard chicken keeper or a homesteader, there are several reasons why you may want to raise your own baby chickens rather than ordering them from a hatchery. Whatever your reason, raising your own chickens not only provides you and your family with sustainable livestock, but it's also a very rewarding and educational experience.

PROS

Save money over ordering baby chickens

A fun 4-H project for kids

Helps keep a fresh supply of eggs

Replace your losses after a predator attack

Opportunities to monetize your flock

Baby chicks are adorable, and you can never have enough!

CONS

Risk of ending up with extra roosters

Raising baby chicks requires you to dedicate a lot of time

Difficult to manage without a broody hen

You don't want more of the same breed that you currently have

You don't have the extra space for a brooder for raising chicks

You don't have room for more chickens

HOW TO TELL WHETHER YOU HAVE A BROODY HEN

Much like every other species in the world, some hens are natural-born mothers and some are not. Certain breeds are known for their broody hens, such as Buff Orpingtons, Silkies, and Cochins, while others, like Easter Eggers, rarely go broody. If your desire is to have your hens hatch and raise baby chicks, you need to start with a breed that is prone to broodiness.

Typically, a hen will go broody once a year. Breeds prone to have broody hens can become broody several times a year. This generally happens when the hen reaches maturity and begins to lay eggs, at 16 to 24 weeks of age.

A good broody hen will hatch out eggs from any chicken, even eggs from other fowl like ducks or turkeys. Hens do not need a rooster present to go broody, but they will need fertile eggs to hatch (see page 66 for fertile egg sources).

Telltale signs that your hen is broody include the hen spending several hours a day in the nesting box, the hen showing aggression when you try to collect her eggs, the hen plucking her breast or belly feathers (she does this to help keep the eggs warm next to her skin), and the hen becoming aggressive toward other flock members (protective momma syndrome).

HATCHING OR INCUBATING EGGS

Whether you're hatching the eggs yourself in an incubator or letting the broody mama hatch out the eggs, there are always tasks that you must do when raising baby chicks. First, I'll go over the pros and cons of letting a broody mama hatch out the chicks and raise them versus hatching them yourself in an incubator. There may be times you want to do both, and I'll discuss that as well.

HATCHING IN THE HENHOUSE

If you let a broody hen hatch out her eggs (or eggs you acquired for her), you are allowing nature to take over with little intervention (and time) from you. Your broody hens will be happy when they successfully hatch a clutch, and you're happy you have new baby chicks to add to your flock.

When you know you have a broody hen and you notice that she is sitting on eggs, you have two choices: (1) Let her stay where she is and hatch them out there; or (2) move her to a protected location specifically for broody hens and their baby chicks. This will be a personal decision you need to make before the babies start to hatch. Moving a hen and her eggs after she's been sitting on them for a while could cause her to abandon her eggs.

If you decide to leave her where she is, other chickens can lay eggs on her clutch when she leaves to eat and drink. To avoid this, carefully mark the fertile eggs with a pencil and remove any new additions from other flock members daily.

There are some risks to the eggs where other chickens are involved. When other chickens lay in the box, they could crush the fertile eggs. And, of course, the nesting box may not be in a safe place for baby chicks to stay once they hatch. For example, in one of our coops, the nesting box was several feet off the floor—way too high for a baby chick to jump out of safely. Keep in mind, too, that monitoring the hen, eggs, and chicks may be difficult if you keep them in the regular coop.

If you decide to move her, relocate her to a smaller coop, dog crate, playpen, or old child's playhouse. Place this temporary coop in a draft-free area protected from the elements. Make sure she has her own food and water and plenty of clean bedding. Move her and her eggs at night when she is calm. When you move her, place her beside the eggs, not on top. She will resettle herself back on top of her clutch.

Be sure to let mama out to free-range and get some exercise if her new coop does not have a run. And keep in mind that there is a chance she may not be happy with her new location and not want to sit on the eggs anymore.

OVERSEEING EGGS HATCHING IN THE HENHOUSE

The last thing you want to do is stress out a broody mama. Try to do all your meddling when she is off the clutch getting something to eat and drink. If you absolutely must check on the eggs when she is sitting on them, try to do so from the back to reduce your chances of getting pecked.

When a hen goes broody and is sitting on a clutch of eggs, you will want to candle them between 10 and 14 days to make sure she is sitting on fertile eggs and so you can discard any eggs that are infertile. You can do this with a powerful flashlight or special candling equipment and a dark room. You are looking for signs of development such as an embryo and blood vessels. All nonviable eggs should be tossed because rotten, bad eggs smell to high heaven and risk exploding. Trust me, you don't want a rotten egg to explode all over your broody hen. Mark the fertile eggs with a pencil and remove any infertile eggs daily when she leaves to eat.

Typically eggs hatch at around 21 days, though some need a little longer. The hen will rotate her eggs several times per hour all day long and will discontinue this process the closer it gets to hatch date. Mama hens are just smart like that. Around day 21, keep an eye and ear out for little baby chicks. Once they begin to hatch you can leave them with the mama or transfer them to a chicken brooder to raise them yourself (see page 74 for the pros and cons of each).

HATCHING IN YOUR HOUSE

For the record, generally speaking, I like a more hands-off approach and to let nature do its thing. However, when it comes to hatching eggs, I enjoy being more involved and hatching them out in an incubator. If hatching your own fertile eggs is the way you want to go, I would recommend starting small and working your way up. You can buy a decent and operable incubator for less than $75.

INCUBATING EGGS

Hatching your own eggs in an incubator is so insanely easy that sometimes I hatch chicks just because I enjoy the process. Not to mention you can never have too many baby chicks, right? Most incubators rotate the eggs for you and have a thermometer to help you regulate the temperature and humidity.

The little one I use is capable of hatching out nine eggs and rotates the eggs once every hour. I initially bought an incubator that did not rotate the eggs, which meant I had to rotate them every two hours for 18 days. I'm not a fan of anything that manipulates my entire schedule like that, so I quickly purchased another one that did the rotating for me.

Place your incubator in a location that is free from drafts, not in danger of being knocked off the counter, and in a place that you walk by at least once a day. You don't want to set up your incubator and then forget to add water or fail to notice the power went out. Typically, incubators need to be between 99 and 102 degrees Fahrenheit with a humidity level of around 50 to 55 percent. Failure to maintain temperature and humidity can result in health problems and deformities in the chicks. Depending on your incubator, you will need to add water and stop the rotation process around day 18. From day 18 to the hatch date, the chicks are getting into position and no longer need to be rotated.

THE HATCHING

When incubating eggs, understand that some will not hatch. A 100-percent success rate is rare. Candling (as I described on page 71) will help you see how many developing eggs you have, but even then, some may fail to develop all the way to maturity.

Around day 19 to 21 of the incubation process, you will begin to hear little pips. These pips are the baby chicks working their way to the outside world. As tempting as it may be, don't try to aid the baby chick in getting out of the shell. There are several reasons why you don't want to help a chicken break free. First, the hatching process is exhausting, and the chick needs to rest between bursts of energy. This is normal, and the little chick should not be rushed. Further, the membrane may still be connected to the chicken, and preemptively removing the shell could injure it. Finally, a chick who cannot escape their own shell could be genetically inferior or have health issues. Helping them get out could prolong their suffering.

CARING FOR NEWBORN CHICKS

Before you plan to hatch your first egg, with either a broody mama or an incubator, you need to decide whether you're going to raise the chicks yourself in a brooder or leave them with mama. The plus side of raising chicks in a brooder is that you can control the temperature and environment and can keep the chicks safe from exposure to predators and bullies. Furthermore, raising chicks in the brooder allows you to have lots of interaction with the cute fluff balls. Of course, raising chicks yourself in a brooder is a big investment of your time and energy. Maintaining a brooder in your home takes up space, costs money, and can introduce a dusty mess into your house. These are all factors to weigh as you make your decision.

On the other hand, the decision to leave the chicks with mama hen to be raised in the coop has its own set of pros and cons. On the plus side, mama takes on the time and labor to raise her babies (rather than you needing to do so). When the chicks are raised by the mother hen, they get a wonderful, balanced diet from an early age by foraging with the flock. Many chicken keepers favor this option as it feels closer to the chickens' natural behaviors. However, it is not safe to assume that every broody hen will make a good mother. Some hens will abandon their chicks after they hatch. There is also more risk of injury to the chicks when they are living in the coop with the flock; their little bodies risk injury when leaving the perches or nesting boxes, and the threat of bullying and predators is ever present. Not every option is a good fit for every chicken keeper and flock. Whatever you decide, weigh your options carefully.

MOVING CHICKS TO THE BROODER

When chickens begin to hatch, it will be tempting to open the incubator and love and cuddle them. However, it is extremely important that the humidity and temperature stay regulated in the incubator. Opening and closing the lid could affect that. When chicks first emerge from their shell, they will still be a little wet.

Whether the chicks are in an incubator or with their mama, you don't want to move them until they are dry and fluffy; then it will be safe to relocate them to the brooder. Before relocating the chicks, make sure your brooder has plenty of bedding, such as wood shavings; that the heat lamp is on; and that the brooder is warm.

The temperature under the heat lamp in the brooder should be between 90 and 95 degrees Fahrenheit. Check your farm supply store for a cheap, small thermometer to place in the brooder. You can adjust the temperature under the heat lamp by lowering or raising the heat lamp. The lower the lamp, the higher the temperature under it; the higher the lamp, the cooler it is. Reduce the temperature in the brooder by 5 degrees Fahrenheit every week until the brooder temperature is the same as the outside temperature.

Brooder Box

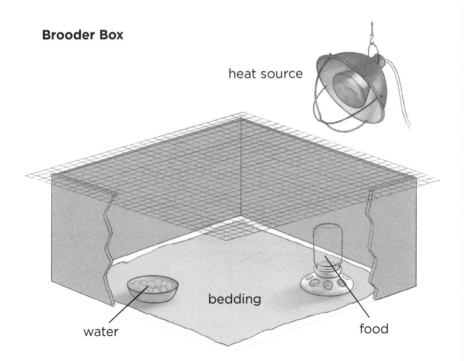

heat source

bedding

water

food

INTRODUCING NEW MEMBERS OF THE FLOCK

For me, going from the brooder to the chicken coop is always a bittersweet moment. Generally, by the time the chicks are ready to move, I'm over taking care of them every day. Between their attempts at escaping their coop, the dust and poop everywhere, and cleaning their water several times a day, I'm ready for the empty nest. However, it never fails that as soon as my brooder is empty, I want it full again with baby chicks.

At my homestead, we have three transitional units for the chickens. We start with the incubator and then move them to the brooder. Between weeks 6 and 10 we have a small grow-out coop (like the one I discuss on page 29). After they are 11 weeks old, we move them to the permanent coop to join the rest of the flock. We have the grow-out coop placed right by the fence of the permanent coop and run, so even at a young age, the chickens can all interact and get used to one another without there being any opportunity for the adult chickens to injure the young chicks.

One of the main reasons you want to keep younger chicks away from the adults is for their safety. Not only do baby chicks need a controlled temperature in their living environment, but they also need a controlled playground, at least until they become old enough to defend themselves. Chickens begin to establish a pecking order almost the minute they hatch. Dropping young chicks in with your established flock would be like sending your kindergarten-age child to high school. They are too young to defend themselves against schoolyard bullies and too immature to keep up with the crowd.

THEY GROW UP SO FAST!

Weeks 1 to 3: Your chicks will be adorable little puffballs who are delicate and fun.

Weeks 4 to 6: Your chickens will be going through that awkward teen stage. Much of their fluff is gone, and they now have feathers. They are nowhere near as cute and adorable as their previous stage but are beginning to look more like chickens.

Weeks 7 to 10: You can begin the transition of moving them into their permanent home and integrating them into your flock.

Weeks 1 to 3   Weeks 4 to 16   Weeks 17 to 21   Week 22 and after

When chicks are fully feathered—a feature that helps them control their body temperature—and resemble the full-grown chickens, they are ready to be integrated into the flock.

When moving chicks, you are dealing with two different issues. This first is that your full-grown chickens and your baby chickens have already established a pecking order within their own flocks. You are getting ready to combine the two flocks into one, which will disturb the pecking order in both. Squabbles and pecking are normal, but keep an eye out for injuries where you may need to intervene. Remove any injured or bleeding chickens and place them in a separate area until they are healed. The second issue is that you are moving the young chickens from the place they've called home, and they will need to adjust and accept where their new home is.

MAKING ROOM

Before you add more chickens to an existing flock, you need to make sure there is plenty of room for the newbies. Remember that for average-size chickens, your coop should include 2 to 3 square feet per chicken, not including nesting boxes. Your run should provide 10 to 12 square feet per bird, although most chicken keepers like to have closer to 25 feet per chicken.

Consider adding some more perches for the new members. Add more waterers and feeders, if necessary. Include some treats from the boredom-busting suggestions on page 38 to distract the chickens. Distracted chickens, especially if you use food they love, will be too entertained to worry about fighting.

HOME IS WHERE THE EGGS ARE

When chickens are moved, they need to be retrained to know where home is. That way they will return to where you want them to at dusk when it's time to "coop up." As I mentioned, we place our grow-out coop next to the permanent coop. We do this for two reasons: so the older flock can get used to the new flock over the course of a couple of weeks and so the new flock can get used to their new location.

When we transition our youngsters into the main coop, we let the older flock outside (or in their run), place the new chicks inside the coop with some food and water, and keep the door closed for the entire day until they are all perched up at dusk. Once the baby chicks (they are more like late teens now) are settled on the perches, we open the coop door and let the older ones in. They are less apt to start fighting when they are tired and ready for bed.

ADOPTED CHICKENS

It may not always be baby chicks you are introducing into the flock. Sometimes you are adopting an older chicken or have bought a full-grown chicken. In either case, if you're adding an outside chicken into your flock, the steps will still be the same.

Remember that chickens can carry disease or become sick; the last thing you want is for a newly adopted chicken to make your entire flock sick. When adding chickens who are fully grown into an existing flock, keep them separated for a minimum of two weeks. Make sure they are using separate food and water dishes and that you don't cross-contaminate anything when feeding. Keep their temporary living quarters close enough that they can see your existing flock but not so close that they can come into contact with one another. After two weeks of quarantine, if your adopted chickens remain healthy without any visible signs of sickness or disease, proceed with integrating them into the coop the same way you would for baby chicks.

CHICKEN MATH

After being around chickens for any amount of time, it's natural to want to grow your flock. Chicken math (a chicken keeper's perpetual need to add to their flock) is a real thing. I tease and call them my little minions; the way they follow me and run to see me every day makes me feel like I'm their Chicken Queen. Who wouldn't want a flock of followers who worship them? Well, maybe worship is a little strong, but they do follow me everywhere I go, they are great companions, and they supply me with breakfast every day. Of course I want more, and I bet you do, too. But how many is too many?

First you need to find out your local laws. Hopefully, this is something you did before getting chickens in the first place. If not, I don't tattle, but now is the time to look those laws up. Many areas, especially urban ones, have restrictions on the number of chickens you can keep, as well as restrictions regarding roosters. At our coastal homestead in South Carolina, it was illegal to own roosters, and depending on which side of the street you lived on (literally), it was either legal or illegal to own chickens. So do your homework and read the fine print.

Once you've read and understand your local laws regarding poultry restrictions, you need to determine whether you have the room. Chicken runs need a minimum of 10 to 12 square feet per bird. Larger breeds need more living space than smaller breeds. For instance, Jersey Giants can weigh close to 15 pounds, while bantam breeds weigh closer to 2 pounds. The bigger the breed, the more space they'll need to roost and live. If you are expanding your coop as well as your flock, make sure to check with local building codes and your HOA requirements, if they are relevant.

Something else to keep in mind is the life span of your flock. Yes, chicks are fun, adorable, fluffy, and addictive, but they'll also live up to 10 years, so make sure you are prepared for the lifetime commitment.

CHAPTER 5

KEEPING YOUR HENS (AND ROOSTERS) HEALTHY

As chicken owners and enthusiasts, it is our responsibility to provide not only for their happiness but also for their physical well-being. In this chapter, I'll cover how to handle chicken sickness and injury, as well as when to call the veterinarian and what to do at the difficult moment when there is nothing more to be done.

SIGNS OF A HEALTHY CHICKEN

Spending time with your flock daily will be your first step in preventing problems. Prey species like chickens often instinctively hide their sickness because they don't want to seem like an easy meal for predators. This may be a great survival aid, but it makes it hard for us as caretakers to know when something is wrong. This is why being able to recognize the signs of health is just as important as recognizing the signs of sickness; noticing that a sign of health is missing could be the key to spotting a problem.

As an experienced chicken keeper, many of these signs are already familiar to you. Use this list as a handy reference to remind yourself to observe your flock for signs of health.

Eggs. Hens who are of egg-laying age should produce eggs with shells that are hard to crack and that are uniform in size.

Combs and wattles. They should be bright in color (red to bright pink), soft, and pliable. The exception would be if you are raising a breed with a different-color comb, such as an Andalusian. In that case, know the color of the healthy comb and keep an eye out for any change.

Plumage. Feathers should be whole and glossy or shiny, except when the chicken is in molt. Feathers should rest close to the body, except when the bird is dust bathing, mating, crowing, or fighting.

Eyes. They should be clear and free of matter or drainage.

Beak and nostrils. The beak should be complete, not chipped, broken, or crossed. Nostrils should be flat, not puffy, with no drainage.

Breathing. Chickens should breathe with their beak closed unless it's very hot. Their breath should have a regular rhythm and should not be fast-paced.

Crop. The crop is at the base of the neck and is a part of the chicken's esophagus. They store their food there while it waits to be digested. When the chicken has just eaten, you can feel a large lump in the front that is a little bumpy from undigested food and grit or gravel. They will digest their food daily. If the lump persists for more than a day, see the details about an impacted crop (page 91).

Legs and feet. Your chickens' legs, feet, and toes should be smooth and soft. The bottoms of their feet should be pliable. They should walk without a limp.

Vent and stool. Chickens poop, lay eggs, and urinate all out of the same location, the vent. They shouldn't have any poop attached to their vent or the surrounding feathers. Their stool should be a soft brown or green, sometimes yellowish, with a white top. The color may vary depending on what they eat. Their stool is mixed with their urine, so it will be the consistency of soft-serve ice cream.

Weight. Chickens should be plump. Their weight varies from breed to breed, with an average of 5 to 8 pounds. Larger breeds weigh up to 12 to 15 pounds, while bantam breeds can weigh 4 pounds or less.

Appetite. If chickens are awake, they should be searching for something to eat. Rarely will a healthy chicken turn down the opportunity to eat, especially if the food is worms.

Behavior. Chickens should be active, alert, and with other members of their flock.

SIGNS SOMETHING IS WRONG

Use this list to help you identify when something might be up with your bird. When you notice something is wrong, take immediate action; it could be a matter of life or death.

EGGS

A chicken's egg can tell you a lot about the health of your hen. Eggs should have a hard, uniform shell that is difficult to crack, and their yolks should be a rich, golden yellow or orange. The following examples are ways that eggs differing from that healthy standard might indicate a problem.

Fragile shells. Shells that break before you can intentionally crack them or shells that break apart as you crack them generally mean your chicken needs extra calcium or better nutrition. Offer your bird some plain yogurt, crushed oyster shells, or ground eggshells, as well as probiotics.

Rubber eggs or shell-less eggs. Chickens need calcium to produce eggs. Lack of calcium can lead to thin eggshells or no eggshells at all, in which case you'll have a rubber egg. Other factors that may contribute to rubber eggs are young chickens new to laying eggs, old chickens at the end of their egg production, or a viral or bacterial infection. Offer crushed oyster shells or crushed eggshells to your chickens if they show signs of needing more calcium.

Lash egg. A lash egg is a round mass that resembles an egg but is rough and bumpy and contains layers of tissue and pus. It's a result of an infection in the oviduct system and usually requires antibiotics.

Egg bound. Hens become egg bound when an egg is trapped inside an oviduct. If not treated or resolved, it could lead to death. Signs of an egg-bound hen include (but are not limited to) lethargy, swollen vent, reduced appetite, diarrhea, shaking or straining, depression, or a faded comb. If your hen is egg bound, try soaking her in warm water for several minutes at a time or applying a personal lubricant or Vaseline to the vent with a cotton swab. Be careful not to break the egg inside her, as this can cause serious damage.

COMBS AND WATTLES

Combs and wattles should be red to bright pink, unless you have a breed with an off-color comb. Another reason for a pale comb is age; young birds who haven't hit maturity have pale combs. A light pink, white, dark red, or purplish comb is a sign that something is wrong.

Pale comb. This can indicate a plethora of issues, including anemia, lice, parasites, malnutrition, being egg bound, or suffering from heatstroke, dehydration, or coccidiosis.

Purplish, blue, or dark red comb. This can be an indication of stroke, heart attack, frostbite, tuberculosis, or avian flu.

Spots. You may notice dark spots on your chicken's comb. Most of these will be nothing more than dried blood from being pecked by other chickens. However, rust-colored crusty spots could be an indication of fowl pox.

PLUMAGE

Feathers that are missing, dull, or ruffled can be signs of sickness, although there are reasons for missing feathers that do not indicate illness. These include mating (missing feathers on the back), fighting, laying on eggs (a hen will remove her chest feathers to keep eggs warm), molting, or a change in diet. If you have eliminated these causes for missing or dull feathers, this might indicate a problem. Possibilities include depression, stress, mites, parasites, lice, and vent gleet.

Chicken feathers are covered with an oil that helps keep them insulated and protected. When the oil dissipates and feathers break, it's time for some new feathers—molting. During the molting season, there will be so many feathers on the coop floor and in their run, you will think something came and killed one of your chickens. Chickens in molt will also look kind of pathetic and haggard with naked skin. Offer your molting chickens some probiotics and protein such as mealworms to help support their immune system while it is focused on feather production.

EYES

People say that eyes are the windows to the soul. With chickens, the eyes are the windows to their health. Signs of eye problems include inflamed eyes, discharge, cloudy eyes, swollen eyes, or a closed eye or eyes. These issues may be caused by a variety of factors, including a viral or fungal infection, fighting or pecking, a respiratory infection, an insect bite or sting, or a vitamin deficiency.

Many times, an eye issue can be rectified by rinsing the eye with a gentle wash of warm (not hot) water and using medicated drops or prescription drops from your veterinarian. If the chicken is being pecked on, remove them from the flock until they can recover.

BEAK AND NOSTRILS

Chickens rely heavily on the use of their beaks for eating, drinking, grooming, communicating, protecting, and more. Chickens with deformed or injured beaks can have trouble eating and drinking, establishing pecking order, and defending themselves. A healthy beak should be uniform, smooth, and without cracks or breaks. The following signs may indicate a problem.

Scissor beak (aka cross beak or crooked beak). All of these terms describe a congenital problem where the top and bottom of the beak don't line up. This is a genetic issue that often worsens with age. Problems with eating and drinking can result from a scissor beak, leading to starvation or dehydration. Though culling or seeking an avian veterinarian is recommended, it is possible to successfully raise a chicken with scissor beak without medical intervention; I speak from personal experience. We kept a close eye on our scissor-beaked girl, gave her deep food dishes so she didn't eat off the ground, monitored her weight, and watched to make sure that she consumed water. She lived a long life on our homestead.

Parrot beak. This happens when the upper beak grows longer than the bottom beak or the bottom beak is too short. In either case, you may need to trim or file your chicken's beak. (See How to Trim Beaks and Toenails on page 99.)

Underbite. Debeaking (clipping the top beak to prevent pecking) can cause an underbite, as well as chronic deformities. You may be able to file the lower beak (see How to Trim Beaks and Toenails on page 99) to help encourage normal growth.

Metabolic disease. This kind of illness causes fast growth in the beak and nails, often resulting in a lack of nutrients and a dull or weak beak and nails. Several fast-growing breeds, such as broilers, are prone to metabolic disease. Increased nutrition and vitamins, as well as trimming the beak, may help.

Broken beak. Beaks can break for several reasons, including getting caught in a fence, fighting, pecking a hard surface, or the chicken having a brittle beak. If the beak is just cracked and the tissue underneath is not exposed, as if you broke your nail below the quick, you can repair the crack with some superglue and an empty tea bag. The tea bag serves as a repair patch, just like one you might glue to an inflatable raft. Empty the contents of the tea bag, and then cut the bag to the size of the crack. Apply a tiny drop of superglue on top of the tea bag patch to seal it to the beak. If the break has exposed the tissue and is bleeding, you will need to stop the bleed with a tissue or blood stop, clean it with warm water, treat it with an antiseptic spray, and continue to do so three times a day until the beak is healed.

Discharge from nostrils. Dirty nostrils are normal, especially if your chickens are foraging in the dirt for worms. However, nostrils that have discharge are a sign of infection and need to be treated.

BREATHING

Your chickens' breathing should not be labored. Wheezing or coughing could be signs of parasites, a lung infection, or respiratory disease. Symptoms of respiratory disease also include swollen nostrils and eye discharge. All respiratory problems should be handled by a veterinarian. Make sure your coop is well ventilated to allow fresh airflow and help prevent breathing issues.

CROP

The crop is a kind of holding tank at the bottom of the chicken's esophagus that stores the food until it's ready to be transferred to the stomach. Signs that it is not emptying properly include weight loss, lethargy, and strange head movements.

Impacted crop. This happens when the food is stuck in the crop and doesn't go to the stomach to be digested. This is uncomfortable and can cause serious health problems. To treat an impacted crop, use an eyedropper to give your chicken a couple drops of olive oil or cod liver oil down the throat in the morning and then gently massage the crop. If the impaction does not go down after three days of treatment, see a veterinarian for possible surgical removal.

Sour crop. When undigested food left in the crop starts to ferment, it causes a buildup of yeast. It's basically like thrush in humans—a yeast infection in the mouth. Chickens with sour crop will have foul-smelling breath and may still have impacted food in their crop. To prevent and treat sour crop, clean water feeders daily and add apple cider vinegar to the water. Give the chicken probiotics, including plain yogurt, but otherwise limit "people food."

LEGS AND FEET

Remember that legs, feet, and toes should be smooth and soft and that the bottoms of your flock's feet should be pliable. Here are some common leg and foot issues.

Scaly leg mites. These are small parasites that burrow under the scales on the chicken's legs. They create crust and deformities on the legs and toes. Mites travel from chicken to chicken via their perches; cleaning perches can help prevent the mites from spreading. The suggested treatment for leg mites is to spray the legs three times a day with VetRx and then rub coconut oil, linseed oil, or vegetable oil into the legs and feet to smother the mites.

Bumblefoot. This is a bacterial infection that causes a dark-colored abscess on the padding on the bottom of the foot. If left untreated, it can lead to lameness. To treat bumblefoot, soak the foot in warm water with dissolved Epsom salt (½ cup salt per 1 gallon water) for several minutes to soften the scab. Remove the scab covering the abscess and use tweezers to remove the core, which looks like a whitish thorn. Spray with antiseptic spray, cover with gauze, and wrap with first aid tape. When you have wrapped the foot, keep the chicken in isolation until they can walk comfortably.

VENT AND STOOL

A chicken's vent is where the eggs, poop, and urine all come out—one hole does it all. The poop should be the consistency of soft-serve ice cream and green, brown, or yellowish with a white cap—unless it's a cecal poop. A cecal poop will occur every 8 to 10 stool movements and will be runny and smelly, sometimes a different color than the normal stool. The cecal poop is the chicken's way of doing spring cleaning in their bowels. If their stool doesn't look healthy, the underlying cause might be a change in diet, stress, worms or parasites, a broken egg inside the chicken, or vent gleet.

VENT GLEET

Vent gleet is when a chicken's vent becomes swollen. They will have a yellowish discharge that sticks to the feathers surrounding the vent, like pasty butt in baby chicks but bigger. In addition to the messy behind, chickens suffering from vent gleet may have a bloated abdomen, gas, decreased egg production, and dull feathers. Vent gleet can be caused by stress, parasites, a pH imbalance, or a bacterial, fungal or viral infection.

To treat vent gleet, isolate the chicken until they are feeling better. Offer the chicken free grit and clean their water feeder daily. Clean their rear with a warm, damp towel and trim the surrounding feathers. Apply an over-the-counter antifungal cream to the vent. Feed the chicken probiotics, but avoid human food or treats. Deworm with a medicated dewormer.

WEIGHT

If your chicken is losing weight, it could be a sign of sickness. Possible reasons for weight loss include being at the bottom of the pecking order, depression, stress, being egg bound, or suffering from an impacted or sour crop, parasites, worms, vent gleet, or malnourishment.

WORMS AND PARASITES

If you have chickens, you'll have to deal with worms and parasites, no matter how pristine your coop and chicken run may be. All it takes is one wild bird flying overhead and pooping on the same ground where your chickens roam to introduce a parasite to your flock.

EXTERNAL CHICKEN PARASITES

Parasites can make your chicken miserable, not to mention sick, because they feed on the blood of your chicken and can cause anemia. Common external parasites include mites (like the chicken red mite, northern fowl mite, and scaly leg mite) as well as fleas, bedbugs, and lice. Symptoms of an external parasite infestation may include pale wattles or combs, crusty legs, feather loss, over-preening, weight loss, and reduced appetite.

Whenever you're treating for external parasites, it's best to treat the chicken AND the coop. Continue treatment for 21 days to prevent any parasite eggs from hatching. To keep the coop and bedding clean, use cleaning-grade vinegar, which has a high acidic content, to scrub down all surfaces. Oil the chicken perches with linseed oil and add diatomaceous earth to their dust baths. Finally, add apple cider vinegar and a garlic clove to their water.

To treat the chickens, rub olive oil or linseed oil on their legs, combs, and wattles. In a well-ventilated area, being careful that you and the chickens don't inhale too much dust, rub diatomaceous earth all over their feathers, under their wings, and around their vent. Consider over-the-counter medications as well.

INTERNAL CHICKEN PARASITES

Internal parasites can often be diagnosed by examining the chicken's stool with the naked eye or looking at a sample with a microscope. You can take stool samples to your veterinarian as well. Common internal parasites include caecal worm, gapeworm, gizzard worm, roundworm, and tapeworm.

Internal parasites like to live in the chicken's liver and digestive tract, which is why many of the symptoms have to do with digestion. Symptoms include weight loss, reduced appetite, shortness of breath or gasping for breath (with gapeworm), over-eating, undigested food in the stool, diarrhea, bloody stool, pale yolks, parasite eggs or worms in the stool, depression, pale comb or wattle, reduced activity, and, rarely, sudden death.

Worms are most active in spring and summer and are often dormant in the cold or when it's above 95 degrees Fahrenheit. Take the following preventive measures when parasites are dormant, and they will not live to become active.

- Clean up and prevent muddy and wet areas in the coop and run.

- Replace bedding and remove feces regularly.

- Rotate the area your chickens forage on every 30 days or less.

- Keep grass cut short.

- Treat your flock with dewormer from your veterinarian or farm supply. Read all dewormer labels thoroughly, as many are not intended for chickens and some may recommend that you wait for a certain period before consuming the chickens' eggs again.

BEHAVIOR

Healthy chickens are social, active feathered friends, very curious and always on the move. Some behavior issues that may be an indication of health problems include coughing, sneezing, isolation, not roosting with the flock, lethargy, constantly fluffed feathers, or not holding the head up. If you notice one of these signs, look over your chicken to see what other signs of sickness may be present.

Ideally, you will have a wonderful avian veterinarian or farm veterinarian close by. Realistically, that's not always the case. Unfortunately, the supply of chicken vets in the United States has not caught up with the growing number of chicken keepers. Thus, many chicken owners have become their own chicken vet out of necessity.

That said, any time you are uncomfortable handling a situation, believe you can't diagnose the problem, or think your chicken needs a prescription medication, call a vet. Sometimes you can carefully watch your vet perform a task, and this will give you the confidence and knowledge to do it yourself next time. This happened with us when we had to give our three baby goats injections once a day. Because the goat vet was more than an hour away, they were happy to teach me how to do it during their visit.

AVIAN FIRST AID

A well-stocked avian first aid kit is a must if you raise chickens. Because you are already an awesome chicken keeper, it is safe to assume that you have a kit. Here I'll cover some details about your kit and suggest some things you might want to add.

Just like fire extinguishers and the leftovers at the back of the fridge, some things in your first aid kit go bad and will need to be replaced. First aid essentials with expiration dates include probiotics, vitamins, electrolytes, essential oils, other oils like olive oil and cod liver oil, herbs, antibiotics, garlic powder, diatomaceous earth, and dewormer.

You will want to check your first aid kit for dates and supplies once a year. I like to do this task in winter before baby chicks arrive in the spring. At that time, I also check my heat lamps, buy an extra bulb, and clean a spare dog crate for any sick or injured chickens. Buy extra spray bottles and rubber gloves when they are on sale.

WOUND CARE

Unfortunately, much like parasites, wounds are something all chicken keepers must deal with sooner or later. Chickens may injure themselves or be injured by other chickens, dogs or cats, predators, or debris—natural or otherwise—in the yard. Before you begin treatment, make sure you have all your supplies out and are prepared to treat the injury. Your wound care supplies should include:

· Antibiotic ointment

· Antimicrobial spray

· Blood stop

· Blu-Kote

· Blunt-end scissors

· Clean feeder and waterer

· Dog crate with bedding, or some other way of keeping an injured chicken safe and comfortable during recovery

· First aid tape

· Gauze pads

· Headlamp or light

· Hydrogen peroxide

· Iodine

· Old towel

· Rubber gloves

LIST CONTINUES

- Saline solution

- Squirt bottle (for saline solution)

- Warm water

The first step in caring for a wound is assessing the situation. Ask yourself the following questions: Is the wound major or minor? Is this something you can treat, or should you take your chicken to a veterinarian? How deep is the wound? Is it a surface wound that can be treated with dressing, or is it several layers deep and requires stitches? Is the wound so serious that it cannot be treated (in which case culling might be the most humane thing to do)? What type of wound is it? Is it an animal bite? A wildlife or animal attack may require antibiotics to prevent infection.

Once you have answered these questions and feel this is an injury you can treat, move on to the following steps.

1. Clean the wound with saline solution.

2. Spray the wound with antimicrobial spray or iodine and allow it to dry.

3. If the wound continues to bleed, use blood stop to clot the blood.

4. Once bleeding is controlled, apply a thick amount of antibiotic ointment.

5. Cover the wound with gauze, fastened with first aid tape.

6. Transfer your chicken to the recovery area, and provide food and water.

7. Clean the wound and apply clean bandages three times a day.

8. When a scab forms and your chicken is in good health, apply Blu-Kote to the wound and introduce the chicken back into the flock.

HOW TO TRIM BEAKS AND TOENAILS

Generally, a chicken's beak will be kept trimmed naturally as they eat grit, forage, and peck. However, there are cases where you will need to step in and help nature along to keep your bird healthy. If the need arises, you can take your bird to the veterinarian to have its beak trimmed, or you can use a rough-grit nail file to gently file the beak. Some chicken keepers trim the beak to prevent pecking in crowded living conditions. This is not a practice I recommend.

Toenails are much like beaks—they stay trim through foraging and scratching, as well as perching. On rare occasions, you may need to trim your chicken's nails, especially if your chickens don't forage in the yard.

WHAT YOU'LL NEED:

- Bowl of warm soapy water (just a couple of drops of dish soap)
- Paper towels
- Fingernail clippers or pet nail clippers
- Blood stop
- Rubbing alcohol

WHAT TO DO:

1. Soak the chicken's foot in the warm water.

2. Dry the foot with paper towels and remove all dirt, poop, and so on.

3. Trim the nails with the clippers. Be careful to only cut the translucent part. If you accidentally cut too much and the toe starts bleeding, apply blood stop.

4. Clean the clippers with alcohol after every use.

FLOCK MANAGEMENT AND HEALTH RECORDS

Maybe you started your chicken journey with the best of intentions. You have a journal with all your records. You wrote down each birth, how much each bird weighed, and when you wormed them (if needed). Then, as the year progressed, you slowly stopped writing in your chicken journal and now you can't remember where you put it. Sound familiar?

Today is a new day. Get a fresh journal, update it to the best of your ability, and vow to keep good records from this day forward. Good records are an important part of animal husbandry. You need to know when you medicated your flock and with what, the last time you performed health checks, and which birds you have treated for injury. For the serious journal-keeper, you can measure your chicken feed daily and keep records of how much you're spending on feed and care for the chickens versus how many eggs they lay, chicks they hatch, and so on. A friend of mine keeps meticulous records of his meat chickens and knows exactly how much it costs to raise his chickens per ounce!

Try keeping your journal and a pen attached to a clipboard on the wall near where you keep the chicken feed. This way, you see your journal every time you feed your flock and you can make quick notes. Here are some things to include in your chicken journal.

- Date of birth

- Breed(s) of chickens

- Age

- Weight

- Type of feed given

- Vitamins, probiotics given

- Medication given, amount, date, reason

- Eggs collected per day (this will help you track their egg cycle)

- Chicks born, how many hens and how many roosters

- Dates of coop maintenance

- General chicken health observations, performed once a week

- Injury, date, treatment

AGING AND THE LIFE CYCLE OF A CHICKEN

As we all know, raising chickens is a long-term commitment. With an average life span of 5 to 10 years, your feathered flock will be a part of your family for a long time.

When hens begin to lay eggs, they are at their top performance for one to two years. Their egg production begins to drop during year three and falls off a little more each subsequent year until they cease to produce eggs.

But when hens stop laying eggs, they don't become useless! There is a lot of value in an aging hen. When a hen stops producing eggs, you can change her chicken feed from layer to regular chicken feed if she is kept separate from the layers. She can help with pest control, train new arrivals, and keep order in the flock. Older hens are wonderful companions and excellent mamas. Hens who like to go broody can continue to hatch out eggs well past their laying years.

Of course, the older we get, the more ailments we have; hens are just like the rest of us. They ain't no spring chickens anymore! Aging chickens will move slower and can't jump as high. This makes them more susceptible to predator attacks. Add lower perches to your coop for aging hens and make sure they have ample cover so they can get away from predators.

Because older hens don't lay as often as they used to, they are more prone to go egg bound. Aging chickens are also more prone to tumors, such as those caused by Merek's disease and lymphoid leukosis.

WHEN THE TIME COMES

Culling, or humane killing, is a subject no one wants to talk about. However, as caretakers, it is our job to make sure our chickens don't suffer. Far too often, we keep a chicken around because we can't bear the thought of losing them or having to cull them ourselves, making them suffer because of our own needs.

We've given our chickens a good life, and they deserve a good death as well. This means a quick approach to ending their pain. The key in achieving this goal is to be fast and efficient. If you don't feel up to the task, you can hire a veterinarian to perform this service, or you can get help from a farmer friend.

You should consider culling a chicken when they have been injured beyond treatment, are sick and unresponsive to medical treatment or have a chronic illness and risk infecting the whole flock, are too aggressive and have caused injury to yourself or others despite efforts at training, or are born with a genetic disease or deformity that prevents them from living a healthy life.

What you'll need:

- A flexible tube cutter or strong tree loppers

- Killing cones or an empty feed bag

- A plastic tarp

- A 5-gallon bucket

- A length of rope; the size will depend on what you are hanging the bag from, but 10 feet should be enough

There are several methods to cull a chicken, and you may have a preferred way that works best for you. This is the method that we've found works best for us and our chickens.

1. If you're using a killing cone, mount it to a tree or wood post.

2. If you're using a feed bag, cut a small hole in the bottom corner, just big enough for the chicken's head to slide through. Tie the rope to the end of the bag and hang the bag from a tree or post.

3. Spread the tarp on the ground below the cone or feed bag.

4. Place the 5-gallon bucket on top of the tarp, directly below the cone or bag.

5. Place the chicken upside down in the cone or bag. They will calm down and stop moving as their blood drains to their head.

6. Wait for their neck to stretch out.

7. Using your cutters, fully place the neck inside the blade and make a quick, firm cut.

8. The head will fall into the bucket and you can let the blood drain out into the bucket.

If your chicken had a disease, you will want to burn them rather than bury them.

This is the least pleasant part of raising chickens. I hope that you encounter the need for culling rarely, if ever. There are always more good days than bad, but there is no denying that this part stinks.

CHAPTER 6

DOING MORE WITH YOUR FEATHERED FRIENDS

So, you've raised chickens for a year or more, and now you're ready to take it further! Fortunately, there are many levels to raising chickens. First is what I like to call the chicken-hope-to-be: someone who wants chickens, has done tons of chicken research, knows all about chickens from reading online, and may even tell their friends who actually have chickens how to raise them. This person doesn't have chickens but would like to in the near future.

On the second level, you have the beginner backyard chicken keeper. This person has two to five chickens, all with names, and maybe even curtains in the chicken coop. They talk about their chickens like high school best friends, and you never need to wonder how their chickens are doing because they are sure to tell you.

After that comes the chicken math expert. This is the person who has transitioned from beginner backyard chicken keeper to chicken addict, because chickens rule and there are so many breeds and what's a few more added to the flock? This person goes to the farm supply store during chick days to buy a bag of feed and comes home with a box full of baby chicks. Many of you are probably approaching chicken math expertise as we speak.

Then comes the sustainable chicken keeper, the person I'm addressing in this chapter. The sustainable chicken keeper is a chicken addict, is in it for the long haul, and would like to raise chickens not only for pleasure but as a sustainable personal business or as super-duper garden helpers. The sustainable chicken keeper enjoys the company of their chickens and uses them to their full potential.

Spread the word: Chicken levels are a thing. You heard it here first.

GARDENING

Gardening with chickens is a tricky but potentially fruitful business. If you have a garden and have chickens, unless your garden is under high security, it is now your chickens' garden as well. Personally, there are only two instances where I actually enjoy having my chickens even close to the garden: at the end of winter to help me get my garden ready for planting and in the fall when I need help cleaning the garden.

I actually planted my chickens their own garden one year in hopes they would enjoy it so much that they would leave mine alone. I had a better chance at winning the lottery without buying a ticket.

SAFE GARDENING

Something I've noticed with many different species of livestock and that I find holds true for chickens is that if animals are provided with enough food, they will avoid the plants that are not good for them—it's almost instinctive. This doesn't mean they'll never eat a toxic plant; it just means that if you have an oak tree, you probably don't need to dig it up in order to have chickens.

The following plants are toxic to chickens. Keep your chickens well fed and avoid exposing them to these plants as much as possible.

- Azaleas
- Beans
- Boxwoods
- Ferns
- Foxgloves
- Holly
- Hydrangea
- Lobelia
- Nightshade family (potatoes, tomatoes, peppers, eggplant, etc.)
- Oak trees
- Periwinkle
- Pokeweed
- Rhubarb
- Yew

NOT ALL FOOD IS GOOD FOR CHICKENS

While we're discussing what is safe and isn't safe for your chickens to eat in the garden, let's discuss what isn't safe for you to feed them in terms of human food. Many people treat their chickens like feathered garbage disposals. But just because they will eat it doesn't mean they should. The following foods and drinks are toxic to chickens.

- Apple seeds
- Avocado
- Butter
- Candy and other desserts
- Chocolate
- Citrus
- Coffee
- Fried foods
- Green potatoes
- Liquor
- Moldy food
- Onions
- Potato leaves
- Rhubarb leaves
- Tomato leaves
- Uncooked beans
- Uncooked pasta or rice
- Unshelled nuts

If you're using herbicides and pesticides in or around your garden, you risk also poisoning your flock. Those same poisons that were designed to kill unwanted insects and bugs are harmful to chickens, too.

The same goes for rodent poisons. The mice and rats eat the poison, the chickens eat the dead rodents, the chickens get poisoned. Chickens love to eat mice and are an excellent solution to most rodent problems. If you allow your chickens to forage and still have a problem with mice or rats, get traps that don't use poison. Consider opting for humane snap-traps, and make sure to place the traps where the chickens can't get to them.

TARGETED HELPERS

I have a rule on my homestead that every animal (and human) must work toward our collective goals. We don't necessarily have pets; we have little helpers. Every warm body must pull their weight, including the livestock.

Chickens and gardens do not always blend well, unless you want to only grow food for the chickens. Chickens will eat every tomato right before it's ripe for the picking, every juicy watermelon the day before you were going to harvest it, and every pumpkin before you even have time to carve it. They love our gardens almost more than we do. However, that doesn't mean they aren't great helpers in the garden—as long as they help at the appropriate time.

Chickens love to scratch and dig up the soil. They love eating bugs, grubs, worms, and grasshoppers. During the growing season one of their favorite treats are those pesky tomato horn worms. I am more than happy to feed the tomato hornworms that made a snack out of my beautiful tomatoes to my flock. Sweet justice, I say.

You seriously don't need a rototiller when you have chickens around; they do all the work for you. We give our chickens access to our garden site three months before we begin planting.

Sometimes I entice them by tossing mealworms or treats into the garden area. In the fall, when I have cleaned everything from the garden, I remove the protective fencing I use to keep the chickens out all season and let them have a feast. Once they have eaten all the weeds, leftover vegetables, and bugs and pooped all over to add a good measure of manure, we put our garden to sleep for the winter.

You can use electric high-tensile fencing to keep the chickens in (or out of) the garden area, or you can use a chicken tractor. A chicken tractor is a moveable chicken pen with an open or wired bottom so the chickens can peck and scratch. When using a chicken tractor to keep your chickens in targeted areas of the garden, move your chickens over a section of your garden and allow them to work it for a week or more but never longer than 30 days. Then move them to another spot. Continue this rotation until your entire garden area is tilled and ready. Rotating your flock at least every 30 days prevents parasites from getting established in the soil and the soil from being overworked.

PVC Hoop Chicken Tractor

COMPOSTING AND CHICKEN MANURE

One of the many benefits of owning chickens is the free organic manure they provide. Chicken manure is more beneficial to your garden than cow or horse manure. It provides more calcium, nitrogen, phosphorus, and potassium.

However, you don't want it to go directly from the coop to your garden—not if you want a garden anyway. Fresh chicken manure is high in ammonia and will burn your plants if it's not left to compost before use. There are also bacteria and other nasties, like *Salmonella* and *E. coli,* that must be destroyed before you add the manure to your garden.

To destroy harmful bacteria, allow your chicken manure to compost for 90 to 120 days before applying it to your garden. When you compost the manure along with other organic material, it creates heat as it breaks down, killing bacteria and weed seeds, leaving you with a rich, organic compost.

We have a separate composting area that we use for our chicken manure. It has three working bins. One contains compost/manure that is ready to use, the middle bin is still cooking, and the last bin is for fresh manure. We continue the rotation process throughout the year. To compost, add brown leaves, straw, hay, or shredded paper in with the manure. Allow air to circulate through the compost pile and use a pitchfork or shovel to turn the pile once a week.

HOW TO MAKE CHICKEN POOP COMPOST TEA

Chicken manure is high in nitrogen along with several other vital nutrients that plants thrive on. Making your own liquid fertilizer from chicken poop is a ridiculously simple way to give your plants the drink they crave.

WHAT YOU'LL NEED:

- An old pillowcase (one you'll never sleep on again)
- Twine or rope
- Clean 5-gallon bucket
- Water

WHAT TO DO:

1. Fill your pillowcase one-third of the way full of composted (minimum of 90- to 120-day-old) chicken manure.
2. Tie the top of the pillowcase tightly with twine or rope.
3. Place the pillowcase in the bucket and cover with water until it's completely submerged.
4. Put the bucket with the chicken manure, uncovered, in a nice, sunny spot in the yard.
5. Once a day, dunk the pillowcase up and down in the water to help keep oxygen in the water. This prevents bacteria and pathogens from growing.
6. After seven days, drain the water from the pillowcase and pour the contents back into your compost pile.
7. The liquid that remains in the bucket is compost tea. To use your tea, mix one part tea with three parts water and use it to water the base of your plants. Avoid using your compost tea on edible leaves.
8. Wash all produce thoroughly before consuming.

THE BIRD BUSINESS

Having the opportunity to make money with your chickens is an added bonus and really helps cover some of the costs of raising them. Chickens paying rent, I like to call it, when you've been able to monetize your chicken hobby and your chickens are earning their keep—maybe even making you a little extra cash on the side.

Before you begin to monetize your homestead or backyard chicken hobby, check with your local and state laws for rules and restrictions. What is legal in my state may not be legal in yours.

Okay, now let's get down to the good stuff—making money from and with your flock. There are many business options when it comes to your chicken flock. Those options might include selling eggs for eating, fertilized eggs to others interested in keeping chickens, and birds themselves, including baby chicks, extra roosters, or laying hens. You may also sell things your flock leaves behind; feathers are popular for art supplies or fishing tackle, and fellow gardeners may be thrilled to purchase your chicken manure fertilizer. Your knowledge as a chicken keeper is valuable as well. Consider teaching classes, writing about your experiences, or building perches, coops, tractors, or feeders. Finally, entering your top chicken in fairs or contests is another fun idea.

You really can let your imagination run wild. The main thing is not to place all your eggs in one basket. Diversify. If your only income is selling eggs and your hens quit laying, there goes your income. However, if you're selling eggs, teaching classes, and building coops, you're still making money even if one source of income falls a little short.

SELLING EGGS

Selling eggs is a great idea if you have a customer base or can create one. When we lived by the beach in a tourist town, I had a waiting list for my girls' eggs. Demand was high, and I priced my eggs accordingly. Then I moved to the country, where everyone and their brother has chickens. Heck, sometimes I even see chickens hanging out at the gas station parking lot. Now I can't even give our eggs away. So we raise just enough for us and give the rest to the dogs. The moral of the story? Find your customers *before* you increase your flock to sell eggs.

After you have checked the laws and are in compliance with your state, be creative in terms of where you look to find your customer base. Local co-ops and farmers' markets are a great place to start. You may want to contact local health food stores, small grocery stores, or other mom-and-pop natural food establishments. Because fresh eggs are so nutrient-rich and tasty, local restaurants, personal trainers, or nutritionists might be interested in your product. Finally, put the word out with local crunchy momma groups, 4-H clubs, and church bulletins. Word of mouth is always the best form of advertising. Connect with people and build relationships; your happy customers are sure to tell others about you.

To prepare your eggs to be sold, you will need to wash them, size them according to your state's laws, and refrigerate them. Eggs should be clean and free of any poop, hay, bedding, and feathers. A great way to keep the eggs clean is by making sure the nesting boxes are clean and have plenty of fresh bedding. Clean landing pads make for clean eggs.

Collect eggs twice a day to ensure they are fresh. This will also prevent any fetuses from developing if the eggs happen to be fertile. Always label each carton with your name, address, and date. To sell eggs, you will need to purchase new egg cartons. Most farm supply stores sell new cartons, or you can order them online.

PRICING YOUR EGGS

When pricing eggs, remember that you are running a business. Your eggs should cost no less than the most expensive eggs at the grocery store. Do not compare your eggs to the cheap eggs at the grocery store—they are apples and oranges. One, your eggs are fresh. Two, your chickens have not been raised in a factory farm where they never touch the ground or see the light of day. Three, you pay a lot more for your one bag of feed than the commercial farms pay for their feed. Four, your time and care for your chickens are valuable. Consider your pricing carefully; don't price yourself out of the market, but don't give the eggs away, either.

ORGANIC CERTIFICATION

Organic certification is ideal if you want to go big and sell commercially. However, the certification process is expensive and laborious. In my opinion, if you're raising chickens on a small scale, you will never recoup the investment sufficiently to make it worth your time. When I was selling eggs, I built a relationship with my customers and they trusted me. They knew how I raised my chickens and were completely satisfied with my natural, farm-fresh eggs. They didn't need the organic label to know they were good.

SELLING CHICKS

Selling chicks, laying hens, or extra roosters can be a great option for monetizing your flock and for solving issues with your flock balance. If you are interested in selling chicks or adult birds, research local laws carefully. Regulations on selling live animals vary greatly from place to place. Do your homework!

TAKING IT TO THE NEXT LEVEL

Consider sharing your passion and love for chickens with others by offering classes or posting regularly online. So many traditions have been lost over the generations and raising livestock is one of them, especially if you live in an urban area. You can set up a table at the farmers' market and bring a couple of your chickens in a cage, dress up with a farmer's hat, and share your knowledge and love of chickens with others. Children especially love petting chickens and asking questions. You can even sell your eggs at the market, along with any other chicken-related items you have or make. It seriously can become a nice little side job that you'll enjoy.

Take the example of the Chicken Lady, a legend at the amusement park not too far away from our home. The Chicken Lady has been with the company for 30 years. She delights children of all ages, who love her chicken talk, chicken songs, rubber chickens, and chicken feathers. She spreads joy to others by sharing her love of chickens.

Yes, raising chickens is work, but it's rewarding on so many levels. It's an investment of your time that offers great returns during the journey. It is each chicken lover's choice how they want to care for, spoil, and have fun with their flock. Hopefully, this book has helped you learn some more about your feathered friends and how you can take this hobby (or way of life, as the case may be) many years down the road.

USEFUL TERMS

autosexing—chicks who can be easily sexed as male or female at hatch due to markings on their heads or backs

avian influenza—also "avian flu," strains of the influenza virus that primarily infect birds

bantam—any small variety of chickens, sometimes referred to as miniature

biosecurity—a set of measures designed to protect your property and your animals from the entry and spread of diseases and pests

breed—a group within a species that has a distinct appearance, resembles one another, typically developed by deliberate selection, and can breed true

brooder—a heated mini coop or container to raise baby chicks

broody—a physiological and behavioral change in hens when they want to hatch chicks

bumblefoot—a bacterial infection of the foot, most commonly caused by staphylococcus bacteria

candling—a process of shining light onto an egg to determine if a fertile egg is developing

chicken math—a chicken keeper's perpetual need to add to the flock

chicken tractor—a mobile chicken coop and run

cloaca—an opening for the chicken's digestive, urinary, and reproductive tracts; the opening is used for eliminating waste and for laying eggs

clutch—a group of eggs

cockerel—a young male rooster

comb—fleshy growth on the top of a chicken's head

coop—a small weatherproof house that keeps your chickens safe and secure while they sleep and lay their eggs

crest—extra fluffy feather growth on the top of a chicken's head; it looks like a fancy hairdo (Polish chickens are an example of a crested breed)

crop—a muscular pouch near the throat, located above the right breast; it's part of the digestive tract and is used to temporarily store food before it moves to the gizzard

culling—humanely killing an animal

diatomaceous earth—a naturally occurring silica material made from the powdered remains of fossilized diatoms or marine phytoplankton; used as a safe natural insecticide

dust bathing—a behavior characterized by rolling or moving around in dirt to cleanse the skin and feathers of parasites, dead skin, and other irritants

egg bound—the condition of having an egg stuck in the oviduct, or a description of a hen in this condition

egg song—loud vocalization made by a hen, usually after she lays an egg

flogging—when a chicken beats an opponent or a perceived threat with her wings

fodder—feed for livestock

fowl pox—also "avian pox," a viral infection in poultry

free-range—when chickens are kept in natural conditions with freedom of movement and without confinement

gizzard—a muscular, thick-walled part of a bird's stomach used for grinding food; chickens eat grit that helps grind down the food in the gizzard

grit—small rocks and pebbles chickens need to consume to help grind down their food

hackles—feathers on the back of a chicken's neck

hardware cloth—a type of welded wire mesh

hatchery—a place that sells chickens, baby chickens, and/or fertilized eggs

incubator—an enclosed apparatus with a controlled environment made for hatching eggs

keel—a ridge along the breastbone to which the breast muscles are attached

layer—a hen that is of age for egg production

mites—miniscule external parasites that may live in water, in soil, or on plants; species of mites commonly attracted to chickens include chicken red mites, northern mites, and scaly leg mites

molt—shedding old feathers to make way for new ones

nest boxes—small compartments inside a coop that offer a quiet, safe place for a hen to lay eggs

nest wars—when hens squabble over the same nest box

parasite—an organism that survives on or in a host organism and gets its food at the expense of the host; common internal parasites in chickens include caecal worms, gapeworms, gizzard worms, roundworms, and tapeworms

parrot beak—a beak deformity in which the bottom half of the beak is much shorter than the top

pecking order—the hierarchy of your flock

pullet—a young hen

roost—perches for your chickens to rest and sleep on

rooster—an adult male chicken

run—a fenced-in or enclosed outdoor space you provide for your chickens

scissor beak—also "crooked beak" or "crossed beak," a beak deformity in which the top and bottom beaks do not properly align

scratch—a type of treats or supplements for chickens, usually composed of various grains and seeds; it's not a complete, nutritionally balanced feed

sexing—determining the gender of a chicken

sour crop—a yeast infection caused by the fermenting of undigested food in the crop

sparring—a natural behavior in chickens when they challenge each other for positions in the pecking order

spraddle leg—a condition when one or both of a chick's legs weaken and spread, making it difficult for the chick to walk or stand

squatting—a submissive mating behavior in which a hen places herself in a position to accept mating from a rooster

started bird—typically, a chicken older than two months of age who no longer requires the extra care of a baby chick

tidbitting—mating behavior of a rooster, characterized by repeated vocalizations (a food call) while picking up and dropping a bit of food

vent—see *cloaca*

vent gleet—also "cloacitis," an infection of a chicken's vent; typically seen in laying hens

wattle—loose, fleshy skin that hangs from the neck of a chicken

RESOURCES

Common Sense Home

» Lots of chicken information here, including reviews of books about chickens, recommended suppliers, and links to other blogs and resources.

» CommonSenseHome.com/homestead-chicken-resources

The Farmer's Lamp

» This site shares information on a wide variety of topics related to more sustainable and self-sufficient living, including livestock care, homesteading, and recipes. There's a great section on raising chickens.

» TheFarmersLamp.com/chickens

My Homestead Life

» This is my website, and you'll find all kinds of info about chickens here as well as herbs, homesteading, and living off the grid.

» MyHomesteadLife.com/chickens

Oak Hill Homestead

» The author of this site keeps chickens and goats and offers great advice about gardening and simple, self-sufficient living.

» OakHillHomestead.com/2017/12/12-chicken-questions-and-answers.html

The Self Sufficient HomeAcre

» A site by Lisa Lombardo, the author of *The Beginner's Guide to Backyard Homesteading*. You'll find information about chicken keeping, farming, cooking, preserving foods, and many aspects of self-sufficient living.

» TheSelfSufficientHomeAcre.com/category/farm-field/livestock -pets/poultry

Timber Creek Farm

» You'll find sections here on chicken keeping, beekeeping, rabbit care, DIY projects, and homesteading as well as some great recipes.

» TimberCreekFarmer.com/category/chickens

REFERENCES

CHAPTER 1

Backyard Chickens. "What Is the Pecking Order and Why Is It Important?" January 19, 2013. BackyardChickens.com /articles/a-guide-to-understanding -the-chicken-pecking-order.64752.

Farm Animal Report. "31 Ways—How to Get Chickens to Stop Pecking at Each Other." Accessed January 23, 2021. FarmAnimalReport.com/2020/05/15/31 -ways-how-to-get-chickens-to-stop -pecking-at-each-other.

Huber-Eicher B., A. Suter, and P. Spring-Stähli. "Effects of Colored Light-Emitting Diode Illumination on Behavior and Performance of Laying Hens." *Poultry Science* 92, no. 4 (2013): 869–73. DOI.org/10.3382 /ps.2012-02679.

Jacob, Jacquie. "Normal Behaviors of Chickens in Small and Backyard Poultry Flocks." The Poultry Extension. Accessed January 23, 2021. Poultry.Extension.org /articles/poultry-behavior/normal -behaviors-of-chickens-in-small-and -backyard-poultry-flocks.

McLeod, Saul. "Maslow's Hierarchy of Needs." *Simply Psychology*. Last modified December 29, 2020. SimplyPsychology .org/maslow.html.

Mendes, A. S., S. J. Paixão, R. Restelatto, G. M. Morello, D. J. de Moura, and J. C. Possenti. "Performance and Preference of Broiler Chickens Exposed to Different Lighting Sources." *Journal of Applied Poultry Research* 22, no. 1 (2013): 62–70. DOI.org/10.3382/japr.2012-00580.

Morton, Nick. "New Studies Examine Effects of Lighting on Chickens." The Poultry Site. April 28, 2013. ThePoultrySite.com /articles/new-studies-examine-effects -of-lighting-on-chickens.

Stayer, Philip A. DVM, MS, ACPV. "Maslow's Pyramid: Self-Actualization for Chickens?" *Poultry Health Today*. June 17, 2019. PoultryHealthToday.com/mobile /article/?id=6695.

Wikipedia. "Five Freedoms." Last modified November 27, 2020. en.Wikipedia.org /wiki/Five_freedoms.

CHAPTER 2

Andrews, Cath. "Lavender Aromatherapy for Chickens." Raising Happy Chickens. Accessed January 24, 2021. Raising-Happy-Chickens.com /lavender-aromatherapy-for -chickens.html.

Bolen, Elaine. "Health Risks of Chicken Manure." SFGate Home Guides. Accessed January 23, 2021. HomeGuides.SFGate.com/health-risks -chicken-manure-98289.html.

Hayes, Bethany. "9 Medicinal Herbs for Chickens to Keep Your Flock Healthier." Morning Chores. Accessed January 24, 2021. MorningChores .com/herbs-for-chickens.

Mile Four. "Chicken Coop Size Calculator." Accessed January 24, 2021. MileFour.com /blogs/learn/chicken-coop-size-calculator.

My Pet Chicken. "How Much Space Should My Chickens Have in Their Run?" Accessed January 24, 2021. MyPetChicken.com/backyard-chickens /chicken-help/How-much-space-should -my-chickens-hav-in-their-H380.aspx.

Ockert, Katie. "Decreasing Daylight and Its Effect on Laying Hens." Michigan State University Extension. October 1, 2019. CANR.MSU.edu/news/decreasing -daylight-and-its-effect-on-laying-hens.

Razorlux Lighting. "Light Bulb Heat Temperature Chart." Accessed January 23, 2021. Razorlux.com/light -bulb-heat-temperature-chart.html.

Rodriguez, Sarah. "Chicken Coop Ventila- tion and Why It's Critical." New Life on a Homestead. Accessed January 23, 2021. NewLifeOnAHomestead.com/chicken -coop-ventilation.

Wieland, Betsy, and Nora Nolden. "Raising Chickens for Eggs." University of Minnesota Extension. Accessed February 26, 2021. Extension.UMN .edu/small-scale-poultry/raising -chickens-eggs.

CHAPTER 3

Joseph, Charles. "How to Easily Determine What Killed Your Chickens." Sorry Chicken. June 21, 2020. SorryChicken .com/how-to-determine-what-killed-my -chickens.

National Park Service. "Black Bear Hibernation." Denali Education Center. Accessed January 25, 2021. Denali.org /denalis-natural-history/black-bear -hibernation.

Pierce, Rebekah. "The Ultimate Guide to Keeping Predators Away from Your Chickens." J&R Pierce Family Farm. Last modified July 2, 2019. JRPierceFamilyFarm .com/2019/07/01/the-ultimate-guide -to-keeping-predators-away-from -your-chickens.

CHAPTER 4

Andrews, Cath. "From Egg Incubator to Brooder: When and How to Move Chicks Safely." Raising Happy Chickens. Accessed January 24, 2021. Raising-Happy-Chickens.com/egg-incubator-to-brooder.html.

Anger, Rachel Hurd. "Is Your Rooster Experiencing Mating Problems?" Hobby Farms. Accessed January 24, 2021. HobbyFarms.com/is-your-rooster-experiencing-mating-problems.

Backyard Chickens. "Using a Broody Hen to Hatch and Raise Chicks." Last modified April 25, 2015. BackyardChickens.com/articles/guide-to-letting-broody-hens-hatch-and-raise-chicks.65989.

Fewell, Amy. "Efficiently Hatching Eggs with a Broody Chicken." Backyard Poultry. May 27, 2020. BackyardPoultry.IAmCountryside.com/chickens-101/efficiently-hatching-eggs-with-a-broody-chicken.

Humidity Check. "Incubator Temperature and Humidity for Chicken Eggs." Accessed January 23, 2021. HumidityCheck.com/incubator-temperature-humidity-chicken-eggs.

Quora. "How Many Eggs Are Fertilized Each Time a Hen and Rooster Copulate?" Accessed January 23, 2021. Quora.com/how-many-eggs-are-fertilized-each-time-a-hen-and-rooster-copulate.

CHAPTER 5

Backyard Chickens. "What a Chicken's Comb Can Indicate." July 2, 2016. BackyardChickens.com/articles/what-a-chickens-comb-can-indicate.72202.

Backyard Chickens. "Wound Care for Chickens." Last modified November 22, 2016. BackyardChickens.com/articles/wound-care-for-chickens.72385.

The Cape Coop Farm. "What to Do with Aging Hens." Accessed January 24, 2021. TheCapeCoop.com/what-to-do-with-aging-hens.

Damerow, Gail. "A Guide to Recognizing and Treating Chicken Foot Problems." Backyard Poultry. October 24, 2020. BackyardPoultry.IAmCountryside.com/feed-health/a-guide-to-recognizing-and-treating-chicken-foot-problems.

Damerow, Gail. "How to Trim a Chicken's Parrot Beak." Cackle Hatchery. June 4, 2020. CackleHatchery.com/how-to-trim-a-chickens-parrot-beak/. "The Complete Guide to Chicken Parasites." December 17, 2019. TheHappyChickenCoop.com/guide-to-chicken-parasites.

Jackson, Richard, BVMs, MRCVS. "Respiratory Disease in Chickens." Poultrykeeper.com. Last modified November 26, 2019. Poultrykeeper.com/respiratory-problems/respiratory-disease-in-chickens.

Murano Chicken Farm. "The Easiest Way to Cull a Chicken (You Need to Know!)." Accessed January 23, 2021. MuranoChickenFarm.com/2017/06/the-easiest-way-to-cull-chicken.html.

My Pet Chicken. "What Is Vent Gleet and How Can I Treat My Chickens That Have It?" Accessed January 23, 2021. MyPetChicken.com/backyard-chickens/chicken-help/What-is-vent-gleet-and-how-can-I-treat-my-H491.aspx.

Omlet. "How Can You Tell If Your Chicken Has Worms?" Accessed January 24, 2021. Omlet.us/guide/chickens/chicken_health/worms.

Oregon State University. "Metabolic Diseases in Poultry: Is It an Inflammatory Disorder?" USDA. Accessed January 24, 2021. REEIS.USDA.gov/web/crisprojectpages/0204911-metabolic-diseases-in-poultry-is-it-an-inflammatory-disorder.html.

Poindexter, Jennifer. "6 Easy Ways to Get Rid of Chicken Lice in Your Coop for Good." Morning Chores. Accessed January 24, 2021. MorningChores.com/getting-rid-of-chicken-lice.

Poultry DVM. "Crop Impaction." Accessed January 23, 2021. PoultryDVM.com/condition/impacted-crop.

Raising Chickens. "Chicken Eye Problems." Accessed January 24, 2021. Raising-Chickens.org/chicken-eye.html.

Roberts, Jason. "Chicken Poop 101: Everything You Should Know & Look Out For." Know Your Chickens. Last modified April 25, 2020. KnowYourChickens.com/chicken-poop.

Roberts, Jason. "Egg Bound Chicken: How to Identify and Treat It (Tips)." Know Your Chickens. September 22, 2020. KnowYourChickens.com/egg-bound-chicken.

Sanderson, Rebecca. "Chicken Wound Care." Backyard Poultry. July 13, 2020. BackyardPoultry.IAmCountryside.com/feed-health/chicken-wound-care.

Spanner, Andrew, BVSc. "How to Tell If Your Chicken Is Healthy." Walkerville Vet. Last modified November 29, 2020. WalkervilleVet.com.au/blog/tell-chicken-healthy-sick.

Timber Creek Farm. "What Is a Lash Egg? Salpingitis in Laying Hens." Accessed January 23, 2021. TimberCreekFarmer.com/what-is-a-lash-egg-salpingitis-in-laying-hens.

Vetco. "Getting Long in the Beak? Time for a Trim!" July 29, 2014. VetcoNM.com/getting-long-in-the-beak-time-for-a-trim.

CHAPTER 6

Backyard Chicken Project. "What Not to Feed Chickens: 33 Foods to Avoid." Accessed January 24, 2021. BackyardChickenProject.com/what-not-to-feed-chickens.

Barnes, Amber. "Things That Are Toxic to Chickens." The Open Sanctuary Project. Last modified September 25, 2020. OpenSanctuary.org/article/things-that-are-toxic-to-chickens.

Barnett, Tonya. "Garden Plants Toxic to Chickens: What Plants Are Bad for Chickens." Gardening Know How. Last modified April 12, 2019. GardeningKnowHow.com/garden-how-to/beneficial/what-plants-are-bad-for-chickens.htm.

Bolen, Elaine. "Health Risks of Chicken Manure." SFGate Home Guides. Accessed January 23, 2021. HomeGuides.SFGate.com/health-risks-chicken-manure-98289.html.

Fery, Melissa, and Nick Andrews. "Turn Manure Into Compost for Your Garden." Oregon State University Extension Service. Accessed January 24, 2021. Extension.OregonState.edu/news /turn-manure-compost-your-garden.

Helmer, Jodi. "14 Toxic Plants Your Chickens Must Avoid." Hobby Farms. Accessed January 23, 2021. HobbyFarms.com/14 -toxic-plants-your-chickens-must-avoid-3.

INDEX

ACKNOWLEDGMENTS

A special thanks to my mother, Pamela, for showing me how to care for animals and for expressing compassion toward all living things. To my little brother, Robert, just because.

To the members of the My Homestead Life group (Old Paths), for always sharing your wisdom with others. Y'all always answer with kindness and a general desire to educate others who want to do what you do, especially when responding to redundant questions from newbs.

Lastly, thanks to my in-house family: to Morgan, for looking after me; to my tiny inspiration, Linden; and to Timmy, for listening to me talk about chickens for hours on end.

ABOUT THE AUTHOR

Amber Bradshaw loves raising livestock, growing food in her gardens, and living off the grid in the mountains. She teaches others how to become self-sufficient by making things from scratch that are eco-friendly. When she's not with her animals or in the gardens, you can find her writing online.

Bradshaw is the author of *Beekeeping for Beginners*, *The Beginner's Guide to Raising Goats*, and *The Beginner's Guide to Chicken Breeds*. She's a former 4-H leader, blogger, and public speaker. She and her family filmed the building of their off-grid home for the TV documentary *Building Off the Grid: Smoky Mountain Homestead*.

Bradshaw is happy to share her knowledge with others through public speaking and private instruction, as well as online at MyHomesteadLife.com.

Chickens are an essential part of sustainable life on her family's developing farm in the mountains of East Tennessee. Her chickens provide her family with meat and eggs as well as income.